A Survivors' GUIDE FOR GOVERNMENT EXECUTIVES

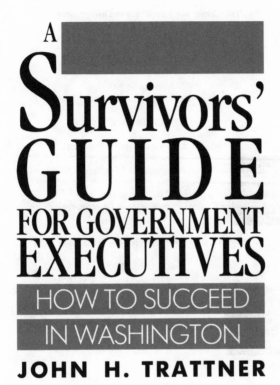

A
Survivors'
GUIDE
FOR GOVERNMENT
EXECUTIVES
HOW TO SUCCEED
IN WASHINGTON

JOHN H. TRATTNER

THE CENTER FOR EXCELLENCE IN GOVERNMENT

UNIVERSITY
PRESS OF
AMERICA

Lanham • New York • London

Library of Congress Cataloging-in-Publication Data

Trattner, John H.
A survivors guide for government executives.
1. Government executives– –United States– –Handbooks,
manuals, etc. I. Title.
JK723.E9T723   1989   353.074'0202   89–5519 CIP
ISBN 0–8191–7430–0 (alk. paper)
ISBN 0–8191–7431–9 (pbk. : alk. paper)

All University Press of America books are produced on acid-free paper.
The paper used in this publication meets the minimum requirements of American
National Standard for Information Sciences—Permanence of Paper for Printed Library
Materials, ANSI Z39.48–1984.   ∞

CONTENTS

FOREWORD

The first months of any new administration in Washington are a difficult time for everyone involved. They are probably toughest for the several thousand individuals to whom the new president has entrusted the senior policy and management jobs in the departments and agencies of government. Many of these political appointees have not been around this track before at this level. They are coming in from outside government and from out of town to take the reins of power. They are people who for a variety of reasons have agreed to take temporary leave of their basic careers--some would say of their senses as well--and serve a tour in the federal government. What have they gotten themselves into?

Washington is many things--a galaxy of power centers fueled by the imperatives of trying to run the country, of politics, and of the pursuit of economic happiness. At its heart is the federal establishment, a noisy, clanking machine responding uncertainly to these dictates. Galvanized by the media; scrutinized and courted by a thousand and one constituent groups and lobbies; probed, analyzed and debated by armies of lawyers and other private-sector professionals, government remains Washington's key dynamic, even as other unrelated factors also push the city's growth and diversity.

Within the close embrace of such a community, it's easy to see why the early period after a change of governments is in a real sense a survivors' game for the newcomers. To the political appointee taking over a senior job, the change of environment is often dramatic and takes place amid intense pressures. It helps to know the right steps to take and the wrong ones to avoid, both at the outset and later on.

Library shelves are loaded with texts about running government and the sad differences between the theory and fact of politics. Two hundred years of the collected musings of political scientists and philosophers are available to students of American government with reading time on their hands. Think tanks, special interest groups, columnists, and other bastions of certitude overflow with prescriptions for the problems Washington deals with, from AIDS to Zaire. And there are the official briefing books, formidable loose-leaf volumes as heavy as barbells, designed to tell newcomers about their agencies and jobs--once they are already grappling with both.

The obvious problem with all these source materials is that none is shaped with the particular needs or schedule of the new appointee in mind. Though investing the time to absorb them will ultimately pay real dividends, it's clear that few appointees can spare that kind of time and energy at the outset. What they need, and quickly, is to get ready professionally and personally for the new job and get on top of it with a minimum of mistakes. In doing so, they don't merely equip themselves to survive the first 90 days. They lay solid foundations for successful performance throughout their time in government.

In these particular needs, there is no better source of advice than those who have already been through the process. People who have served a stint as senior federal managers and policymakers over the past 20 years have piled up an unmatched store of experience and observation in a specific and crucially important sector of the Washington scene. It is the kind of information especially useful for the new political appointee lacking significant first-hand acquaintance with it all.

To tap that rich vein, The Center for Excellence in Government turned to its 400 members, almost all of them veterans of administrations of both parties dating as far back as the administration of Franklin Roosevelt. We gathered dozens of them in small group discussions around the country, with a tape recorder in hand.

It was exhilarating and reassuring to listen as they reflected on their time in office. Their comments reveal a refreshing skepticism and healthy irreverence. But, more important, a great many took away with them a strongly positive sense of having done something worthwhile in Washington and of having achieved to a satisfying degree what they went there to do. Their experience signals the continuing vitality and challenge of the political system they embody. It's a system whose uniqueness rests in part on the ability to spur experienced and intelligent men and women to place their talents, for a time, at the service of the nation.

Distilling some of the best of their collective insights, and passing them along as rules for survival and effectiveness in executive government positions, is what this book is about. Almost all of the quoted material it contains comes directly from those with whom we spoke.

The idea for a survivors' guide was that of Harry Freeman, a founding member of the Center and a steady and solid friend of this and other Center projects. To the Principals of The Center for Excellence who took part in the discussions on which the book rests go deep thanks for the interest and thoughtfulness which they brought to the task.

Gratitude goes also to Center Chairman Bill Morrill for his usual strong leadership, and to him, Vice Chairman Scotty Campbell, and Center Executive Director Mark Abramson for reading through the drafts with a critical and careful eye. Mark also managed the research for the book and oversaw all technical aspects of production. Tamar Osterman did the indispensable work of sifting, assessing and organizing the results of the research with perception and skill. Cathie Faint applied her considerable talents to planning the format and proofreading the text, among other services. Jacque Rouse did the exacting work of putting the text in format and readying it for the camera.

It is all of these people who really made the book possible.

J.H.T.
Washington, D.C.
January, 1989

I

GETTING READY

Chapter Summary

Are you truly qualified to take the job on? Do your experience, training, and skills match its needs?

Why do you want this job? Do you primarily want an opportunity to do something--or only to become somebody?

Are you prepared for the sacrifices and indignities involved?

Are you willing to go the full first-term distance in the job?

Do the job's challenges genuinely interest you?

Are you broadly in agreement with the political objectives of the administration?

Get used to filling out forms and waiting.

Prepare yourself for careful public scrutiny by the Congress.

Expect delays in your confirmation.

Learn as much as possible ahead of time.

Get your personal life in order quickly.

Maybe you're about to take on a senior government job. Or maybe you're only at the stage of thinking about whether to accept the offer of one. Either way, now is your last undisturbed chance to ask, learn, and get ready. Don't blow it.

> "I expected a briefing by the White House on what life would be like in Washington. I expected someone to consider my family and say hey, here's ten realtors, and here's the country club, here's the schools for your kids, and here's some people that would like to meet your wife, and here's the synopsis from the transition team on how to do things. Well, I never got any of that. It was 'sink or swim, pal.'"

Anecdotes like that tell only a small part of the story. Most government executives in Washington don't lead charmed lives. They work hard and long. The rewards while in the job, such as they are, are much of the time intangibles, like personal satisfaction. Even these can be mixed blessings. The pay is likely to be much less than what incoming appointees made in private life, and everything in the capital costs more.

Why, then, does the idea of senior government service remain powerfully attractive? Why would anybody want to do it?

On the simplest level, just the prospect of going to Washington and becoming a part of government raises some pulses. Many people look at it merely as a vehicle to higher salaries and responsibilities later on; this approach is clearly the wrong motivation to government service and is a cynical disservice not only to administration, government and country, but to one's self. On a higher plane, there is the possibility of learning something, of making decisions on a larger playing field, of making a difference in the lives of great numbers of people, of acting on one's beliefs about government and its purpose.

Whatever impulses may bring you into government, preparing for it adds up to considerably more than packing up your old office and heading for the new one in Washington. Gearing up to do the new job is as critical to the administration and the nation as it is to you.

What follows are some of the hard questions to which you'll need realistic answers that you can live with--and by.

Are you truly qualified to take the job on? Do your experience, training, and skills match its needs?

The answers are not as easy as you may think. For one thing, how much do you really know about the job? And what is the source of your information?

Since this is government, not a private-sector firm, you're dealing with a bigger, more layered, more dispersed organization. That means the people who hired you, or would like to, may have only a distant idea of what the job is supposed to do.

> "[The selection] is not made by a board of directors that, on a monthly basis, has been dealing with a given company's problems for years and knows the issues and the criteria, knows the capabilities of the executives who are already there. Rather, it is usually made outside the organization altogether."

Those who selected you may have even less clue about the much more important question of what particular experience, talent, and training it takes to handle the job. All this is information you clearly need to have right away. Only then can you make the vital, realistic judgment whether, in fact, the position fits with your particular background and talents.

On this, a former job-holder offered specific advice that we also heard from many others:

> "Put enough room in your calendar to see all of your predecessors. Have a meeting or two where they tell you what they tried to do. You may discount a lot of it, but it's the best way to learn what's involved in your job."

That's a valuable suggestion, even if time and circumstances don't permit you to see each and every one of these people. Identifying and locating them isn't easy, either. Ask your prospective department or agency, as well as the appointing authorities you're dealing with; they may be able to help. It's clearly worth a strong effort. And after you're in the new job, continue it:

> "Don't assume that your predecessors are your ene-

mies...rely on them as chief early teachers both of
what the job is and who in the (career service) you
can rely on."

Why do you want this job? Do you primarily want an opportunity to do something--or only to become somebody?

If the last question is the one that best describes your interest in a
federal appointment, better think again. A solid case can be made that
the political appointees who do best are those whose careers don't need
a boost from government service.

No doubt there's a certain attraction in a job which comes with some
clout to throw around. More than a few appointees have thought of
government service in precisely those terms--or worse.

"...There's the story about the assistant secretary
who [took an appointment] and his first question
to his staff was 'What days do I brief the President?'"

But you're not being invited in for an ego trip.

"Be sure you know that the government is very big,
and your piece is going to be only a part of it. The
President isn't going to wake up every day and
wonder where you are..."

Nor does government exist to help you increase your marketability,
build your resume, or hike you toward the high six figures in the job you
take afterwards. Some of that in fact may happen. But there should be
no illusions about why people are asked into federal service.

"They're not there for the glory of it. They're there
to serve and understand their role in what they are
doing."

The reality is that you and hundreds of others are being asked to come
in because the administration needs your particular experience and talent,
and views you as reasonably compatible with its political philosophy. For
you, it is an opportunity to fill that need productively in a complicated,
often frustrating environment. It's as simple as that. Taking yourself too
seriously will only lose you respect and friends.

"I've seen a lot of capable people who rise up and

> do a good job in the government in their time there, and then they just destroy themselves because their egos are so far out ahead of their own accomplishments and their own places..."

> "New people coming in think that, at long last, talent has been recognized because they've been picked. And they're not inclined to pay too much attention to what they're told."

Are you prepared for the sacrifices and indignities involved?

You'll wade through time-consuming procedures and formalities that range from irksome to outrageous. You'll encounter attitudes and operating methods that may be strange and cumbersome. At the office, you'll be dealing with big financial numbers but, at home, you may struggle to balance a personal budget that is considerably less than you're used to. You'll forfeit some privacy,

> "If I had known that I had to go through what I had to go through to be confirmed, and had to have my lawyer and my accountant down there working with the President's office and with everyone else, I wouldn't have accepted the appointment..."

and some financial security,

> "There are some major financial sacrifices that these people are going to have to make. I don't think a lot of them realize it...A lot of people we're talking about in these kinds of jobs are at the age where they have kids in college. And the salaries at the top of the government really don't support kids in college, at least more than one. Secondly...I have been blown away by what's happening to housing costs in Washington. Whoever comes in is in big trouble, and ought to understand that up front..."

and perhaps some perks:

> "You're lucky to get a car out of the motor pool when you want it and then when they bring it up, you're lucky if you can fit in it..."

For these and many other reasons, you'll occasionally wonder why you took the appointment in the first place. Wrongly or rightly, others may have the same question about you.

To repeat: The serious answer is that you're there to do a job, render a service, contribute something. Obviously, there can be beneficial personal spin-offs which accrue to some appointees when they return to private life, and a tour in Washington often brings a real sense of accomplishment and enjoyment. Just don't go in with personal advancement as a major goal.

Are you willing to go the full first-term distance in the job?

The average length of stay in senior appointed positions, never very high, has declined consistently over the last 25 years. From about 2.8 years for Johnson's appointees, it fell to 2.6 for Nixon's, to 2.5 for Carter's and to 2.0 for Reagan's.

But those are only the averages. A full third of appointees in the 1967-87 period actually served a year and a half or less--even though it takes at least a year to become really effective in most senior federal executive jobs. As the world in general, and government in particular, grow more complicated, the short-timer has thus become a serious problem for effective federal operations.

Do the job's challenges genuinely interest you?

The position you're focusing on may not be the one in which you can do best, or be happiest in. The federal government may not even be the place for you.

> "Try to understand the job as best you can...But if you're not excited about serving the government, then stay home..."

Are you broadly in agreement with the political objectives of the President and administration for which you'll work?

As noted above, the administration will expect you to be. Within that broad accord, expect to be asked to carry out specific assignments and work toward objectives with which you may disagree to a significant extent.

There are some situations, needless to say, that go beyond this norm.

> "Keep your resignation in the top drawer of your desk. Make sure you're willing to have the guts to use it if your bosses, whoever they may be, try to force you to do something that you really think is unethical or improper in the job or is going to undermine your ability to do the job..."

Don't therefore think of yourself as indispensable, or of your job as something you can't give up.

> "...there's an important principle to state, which is that in any of these jobs you have to be willing to end it tomorrow. If you don't view the job as one that you're willing to leave, without notice, it seems to me you can't do it."

Implicit in this is one caveat. If something you're being asked to do impels you to consider leaving, be sure it's a resignation issue--one on which your disagreement is strong enough to override all other considerations. If it isn't, be prepared to stay on and cheerfully implement whatever it is, despite your disagreement.

As you assemble the answers to these and other questions, you need to know approximately what to expect between the time you accept the offer of a political appointment and your first days in it.

Get used to filling out forms and waiting.

Transitions between governments are always busy. But even at other times in the life of an administration, it's not unusual for an individual who has agreed to be nominated for a position to hear nothing more-- from anyone--for several weeks. What's going on meanwhile?

First, the White House will informally run your proposed nomination by individual senators--those in the leadership, those from your home state, those on committees with oversight of the agency you are being proposed for. A nomination is unlikely to be derailed in this preliminary process. It's a courtesy, and a way of taking some necessary soundings.

Second, the FBI must look at the history of your adult life for any blemishes of character, reputation or associations that disqualify you outright or could at least prove uncomfortable if made public. Known as a full field investigation, this inquiry can be as short as a few weeks or as long as several months. Occasionally, a nomination will be announced before the investigation is complete. The FBI in any case keeps the White House supplied with progress reports. If you've had prior government service, it can speed things up. Be aware that the investigators are quite likely to question your friends and neighbors, who may then call you to ask what's up.

Finally, the White House itself carefully checks a prospective nominee's personal background and financial status. Nominees fill out forms and make personal statements dealing with these matters and may be asked any number of clarifying questions.

Prepare yourself for careful public scrutiny by the Congress.

Unless the various checks mentioned above take an unduly long time, the White House waits until they are finished to make a nomination public. The next required step for most Presidential appointees, of course, is Senate confirmation. First comes the formal public hearing in which you'll be examined by the Senate committee of jurisdiction over your department. Next, after voting whether to recommend approval or disapproval, the committee forwards the nomination to the full Senate. Only if that body approves by majority vote is your confirmation a fact.

Sometimes hilarious, often vexing, a confirmation hearing always needs serious preparation. Here you need and should expect to get some extensive help and counsel from the department you are joining. A hearing can be a quick and perfunctory experience, or long and exasperating, or something in between. Occasionally it can even be fatal. Whatever it is, be ready for it.

The timing of a confirmation hearing depends on several factors. Key among them is probably the relative importance of the job. During transition periods between administrations, Cabinet and equivalent positions usually come first.

Expect delays in your confirmation.

For appointments below the Cabinet secretary level, the possibilities of delay in hearing or confirming a nominee are just about infinite. The White House personnel office, working with the department or agency concerned, must gather and submit a nominee's personal data to the Senate committee. Then there is the committee's own work schedule, and the chance that one or more senators may decide to hold a given nomination hostage in exchange for some concession from the administration, or simply to express displeasure at an administration policy, attitude or action. Such maneuvers may have nothing to do with the nominee in question.

It's therefore not surprising that the hearing or confirmation votes can occur long after you have been nominated. Sometimes even the background investigation won't be complete before your hearing. Not yet being confirmed doesn't prevent you from going to work, getting started on the job and performing many of the routine functions it entails. It does mean that nothing can be done officially, with the force of law and legality, until you are confirmed and sworn in.

> "I was operating the department without being confirmed for two months because the President needed somebody there and the committee was pushing and they (the new administration) couldn't get the reports in. I had a rather complicated financial statement and history and whatnot. They don't have enough FBI men. It's just that simple. They're lined up one after another..."

Before you are confirmed, be careful not to involve yourself, even unofficially or informally, in decisions of substance made by the person you're succeeding, or by the outgoing administration generally, for which you could later be held responsible. Don't, for example, nod your agreement at something that, after you're in the job, turns out to be at odds with your own administration's views.

Learn as much as possible ahead of time.

It is, in sum, an uncertain interim that often follows your initial acceptance of the offer of a federal appointment. But, to repeat, it is also a valuable period for the wise appointee to soak up facts and understanding about the job and the life that's being proposed.

> "It's a good time...to listen and learn. Nobody expects too much from you [in the period before you are actually on the job]. You really have no responsibilities yet. So it's a great opportunity to absorb information about...new responsibilities, to identify what the issues are, to lay out goals and strategies..."

As already seen, there is little by way of organized procedure for general orientation of the majority of incoming appointees. True, most administrations have recognized the need, from a White House level, to make clear where they intend to go and what they expect in that regard from their hundreds of senior appointees. But these intentions have not yet developed into institutionalized procedures.

Your agency, however, will want to brief you on a variety of specifics --about the agency, its programs, your job, the rules on ethical behavior, and the like.

Get your personal life in order quickly.

One of the veterans we spoke with looked at government life in Washington this way:

> "...the first thing you know, if you screw up both
> your vocational and your private life, you're going
> to be a mess. So you've got to keep at least one of
> them stable. Making the transition into Washing-
> ton is one aspect of it."

Before you take over, even before you get to Washington, sit down with your family. Discuss with them the new life style that's about to descend, in particular the demands in time and energy that your job will make on you. With them, examine the available facts about life in the capital--housing, schools, geography. Make some basic decisions about these things that will govern your actual choices when the time comes. Laying down these foundations as much as possible beforehand will avert at least some wrong decisions, misunderstandings, unpleasant surprises, and other kinds of grief. And it will give you that much more time to concentrate on what you're undertaking.

II

THINKING ABOUT PROCESS AND POLITICS

Chapter Summary

In government, you can't operate autonomously.

Get to know the key players.

Monitor the political frequencies.

Keep in constant touch with your interest groups.

Become a better negotiator.

Know when and how to compromise....

...and when not to compromise.

Know where the power centers are.

Never believe anything is over and done with.

Develop a network.

Control your in-box; don't let it control you.

Focus on the difference between thought and action.

Don't think policy making is the exclusive province of political appointees.

Maintain your perspective.

Develop a thick skin.

"You can't take the modus operandi from your
business life and apply it one hundred percent. I
don't know how you can describe all the sets of
differences. But at least the knowledge from the
outset that it's different is important."

That's a good way to approach a senior federal appointment--by truly
understanding that you are going into a different environment with
different ways of getting things done. Some features of the new landscape
will look familiar. Many others won't--and they matter a great deal.

"I've been in this town for 20 years, and am
constantly amazed at how many bright and successful people come here and manage to step into every
mess in Washington. I've seen a lot of really smart
people who really knew the issues but completely
fell on their faces when it came to process. You
can learn the issues pretty quickly if you're smart
about it. But where you get into trouble is on
process."

You'll need to consider these procedural and other differences and be
ready to adapt your operating style as necessary. They not only affect
what you can do in this new job, they often control it.

In government you can't operate autonomously.

"This is a very pluralistic environment and you
don't accomplish anything on your own--no matter
what your powers are..."

It's government by committee. Get used to it. Even routine decisions
in Washington are usually drudged over by several agencies; weeks,
months, even years can go by while a decision stumbles through successive
phases of research and laborious negotiation. Blame it on the intricate
world we live in. Blame it on the less-than-perfect way the federal government is organized. The fact is that almost every goal of government

--and the problems faced in achieving those goals--are the responsibility of multiple agencies. Often, they disagree about how the responsibility is to be apportioned--who gets to do what. The notion of "turf" thus frequently, and often needlessly, delays and complicates the management of government business.

If you're used to pulling the big levers by yourself, sharing that authority with other entities can be a brutal adjustment.

> "People who come into political appointments with no prior Washington experience have enormous culture shock in terms of the multiple points of accountability they have to face...This town operates in a way that's completely foreign to these new appointees. It's unlike the structures they're used to working with. And that's something they've got to learn fast."

Let's take a moment to see what this means.

Imagine a defense contracting company which manufactures a component of the warhead carried by the Minuteman missile. This is not nuclear material, just one part of the warhead casing. To make it, the plant uses milling machinery. These devices grind to exceptionally small tolerances, and some of the company's workers are found to be suffering from the effects of microscopic grains of toxic material produced in the process. When analzyed and measured, the detectable amount of this substance inside the plant exceeds permissible levels. The stuff is being inhaled on the factory floor and it's also going up the stacks and out into the countryside. What's the federal responsibility here, and who has it?

It's not hard to see half a dozen agencies involved. First, the job of overseeing management to bring the situation inside the plant under control belongs to an agency in the Labor Department. Next, possible contamination of surrounding land, air and water resources comes under regulations written and applied by the Environmental Protection Agency; and any legal problems in enforcing those regs will rattle a few in-boxes at the Justice Department (it was at Justice, after all, where those same regulations had to pass muster when they were first written).

What's more, if health problems in the plant result in changes in the manufacture of the casing component, the Department of Energy will be directly concerned. Working closely with the Defense Department, Energy manages the production of nuclear weapons for the armed forces. So it's clear that the Pentagon also comes into this picture. Depending on how the problem is resolved, the State Department and other national security agencies could also get involved. Finally, the Department of

Health and Human Services will need to pay close attention to the entire process.

So much for hypothetical illustrations of the creature the political scientists call multiple accountability. The real thing--in dozens of daily examples--is grist for a busy executive branch mill, one you'll soon come to know and cherish as the "interagency process." And if money or policy is involved--and when aren't they?--you'll find the Office of Management and Budget (OMB) inspecting the end product.

> "The interagency process is critical. In the begin-
> ning of this administration, we wanted an executive
> order to come out. The fellow from OMB comes
> over and we sit down in the basement of the White
> House and he has this stack of papers. I said
> what's all this? Agency comments, he said. I said,
> what the hell does the Department of Agriculture
> have to do with it?...It was, like, the third day out
> of the box, and that's when you begin to under-
> stand a little bit that what you're doing here will be
> a problem there..."

> "You're selling all the time, in the sense of build-
> ing credibility with all those people out there--
> OMB, the Hill, and so on...And you [have to]
> approach them understanding that they have a le-
> gitimate role to play in a democracy, and that your
> job is to figure out how to work with that."

In other words, coalition-building is at a premium in government. But remember that, while some coalitions will endure and function for months, others will dissolve overnight under the heat of a new issue or a new crisis that demands a different combination.

> "You have to build a coalition within the executive
> branch and with Congress to get a policy done...If
> you come in with that recognition, you can be
> effective. Recognize early on the need to have
> people you can talk to on the phone, who have a
> shared interest in a common objective...It's the
> coalition builders who get things done. And
> today's adversary is tomorrow's ally."

Get to know the key players.

> "There are people all over town who can either

help you or hurt you...It's important to get to know
all of these people."

If you're at the assistant secretary level, for instance, there's a long list
of people whose identity and function you need to know--even if you see
or do business with many of them only rarely. First are your contacts and
counterparts in the Executive Office of the President in such areas as do-
mestic and economic policy development, legislative affairs, and national
security affairs. Then there are the central management agencies within
or responsible directly to the Executive Office and with a large voice in
your affairs--the Office of Management and Budget, the Office of
Personnel Management, and the General Services Administration.

There are, of course, your colleagues in other departments whose
missions and duties overlap or mesh with yours; these are folks you'll talk
to every day or twice a week. There are the chairs and members of
Congressional committees and subcommittees and their senior staff
members; representatives of constituent groups, lobbies and other
advocacy groups; and a certain number of reporters and editors. All of
these will zero in on you and take a constant and frequently sharp interest in what you do--and don't do.

By no means least on this list are people in your own agency outside
your immediate office or bureau. Among them are members of the
secretary's and deputy secretary's staff, heads of in-house agencies and
program staff, the legal office, the Congressional liaison shop, general
counsel's office, and public affairs staff.

Monitor the political frequencies.

This is basic common sense in a federal environment where you can't
operate in isolation from the institutions around you. Sure, you've played
office politics before, and maneuvered to get your way. In government
it's a way of life, on a macro scale.

Your goals and your ideas are vital to you. But to get anywhere with
them, you need the respect and support--or at least the assent--of people
in other buildings and other parts of town, not just within your own out-
fit or your own branch of government. So you have to see it from their
viewpoint, too.

"One of the biggest problems I think newly-ap-
pointed executives have who don't come out of a
political background is learning what political
accommodation is all about--what is it the subcom-
mittee chairman really cares about?...Sensitive
political antennae are not by definition corrupting

or bad; they're a set of tools ..."

"The reality is that you have to respond to things that other people think are important...Just because it's not important to you doesn't mean you can ignore it."

But don't think that cohesion and cooperation begin and end with the party team.

"Look, one of your biggest problems is not going to be the civil servants and it's not going to be the Hill. It's going to be the assistant secretaries who are walking in with you, who are in your party, sometime in the first 60 days, who are going to try to cut you off at the knees...An assumption that all political appointees are one big happy family can be a fatal mistake bureaucratically..."

Keep in constant touch with your interest groups.

In tuning to the political frequencies, remember the constituent interests. They broadcast on a highly important wavelength. They are the folks whose farms, labor unions, oil wells, retail store chains, or research projects will be affected by your decisions. Many are well organized and have experienced representatives in Washington.

"Go out and meet all the constituencies. Talk to them and find what they're all about and what their concerns are. And show them that you're concerned."

"One temptation the political appointee has to resist is...staying in the office and listening only to an elite cadre of special assistants. You've got to go out, you've got to have lunch with the lobbying groups...even though you don't have enough time to get everything done as it is."

When you talk with them, however, it takes a bit of skill to know what you're hearing.

"You have to measure the breadth within a particular constituency. You've got to develop some friendships...with people who will tell you what the whole card position is--not just what they're saying, but what they can live with."

Whether you see them personally in groups or individually, or talk to them on the phone, or communicate by letter, be careful to run your interest-group relationships with an even hand.

> "...Interest groups don't trust each other. If you become aligned with any one group more than another and the perception is that you really don't listen to anyone besides certain groups, then your ability to affect those groups will be severely impacted."

Perception, in fact, plays a very big role in how successful you are in Washington--with interest groups as in other areas.

> "In Washington, 80% of your job is perception, 20% is reality. The reality is what you decide and how you decide it and what it really has an impact on. The perception is how you deal with it, and how you reach out to people, and how you try to market it."

But don't forget that Washington is a town of end runs.

> "My agency had [to deal with] a lot of powerful vested interests...You could try as hard as you wanted to get through to those institutions and work well with them and explain what you were trying to do. They responded to it--but up to a point. When that point was reached, they went to the Hill...They had years and years of relationships built up with the chairmen and the [ranking minority members of committees], and you couldn't compete against them..."

That connective tissue between interest groups and veteran members of the Congress is really part of what old hands in Washington see as a three-sided phenomenon--an "iron triangle" whose third leg rests within the career civil service. Ask ten people to describe this relationship and you'll get ten different answers. But in the approximate common view, it is an unspoken but tenacious bond between entrenched elements of the Washington scene that share a number of mutual interests; when necessary, these elements can work together to defend their interests, or to resist initiatives and changes they don't like.

While there is no question that the relationship exists and functions, opinions differ on its significance and impact. You'll have to judge for yourself how much or how little to make of it in terms of your own position and responsibilities.

Become a better negotiator.

Again, you've probably done a lot of bargaining in your time. You'll do more of it in government, and on a wider playing field. You and counterparts in other agencies may have joint responsibility for a given objective. That doesn't mean they share your ideas for reaching it. You're often likely to discover outright opposition to your concepts, or even to the objective itself.

> "...there are always agendas of others who want to do things you don't want to do. They have fairly well-thought-out plans, going in directions you definitely don't want to go in."

Sometimes a department's success in a jurisdictional fight with another agency is what tends to define the project or problem at hand and how it is dealt with. That puts the emphasis in the wrong place--on process at the expense of substance, mostly for the sake just of agency pride or personal self-esteem. It's a battle on artificial turf. And, as with sports played on fake instead of real sod, the damage when it occurs is worse. This kind of struggle eats away at what government can achieve.

> "If you turn that around and say wait a minute-- what is it that we're all trying to accomplish here? And if the other agencies know that's the approach you're taking, you can ameliorate a lot of the turf problem. Keep forcing the focus on substantive issues."

In Washington, more than in the private sector, effectiveness as a negotiator depends on your ability to make others see the legitimacy of your position if not actually to bring them around to it.

> "Frankly, in the federal bureaucracy, government is the art of persuasion..."

It's also the ability to negotiate what's important to you against what's important to others and come out with no one as the big loser and with the interests or policy of the administration served.

Know when and how to compromise...

> "People coming from the business community are used to dealing with black and white situations, where decisions are made based on the merits... [But] looking at it through two administrations, I found that appointees who were able to compromise, particularly in dealing with the Congress, were the more effective."

Obviously, this kind of flexibility is especially valuable when one party controls the White House and the other runs the Congress.

> "...you kind of have to sit in the middle of the avenue and manage both relationships. If you go too far down either end of that avenue you're in trouble. Your job is to be the translator, back and forth, to maintain that credibility on both ends. That can't be done every day, but over the course of a year..."

...and when not to compromise.

Clearly, there will be moments when it is neither advisable nor possible.

> "You have to have the patience to hear them out, then wait them out, then stall them out, and finally say no. The patient, intellectually honest stall is one of the great government ploys."

Know where the power centers are.

> "There are two or three focal points in government whose principal function is to coordinate. When the National Security Council is run properly, for instance, it is a coordinator. The Cabinet group on economic policy became really the key group of people, the key arena, in which economic decisions were made. It was that group you had to convince. You could go at it either through the departments or...the executive secretary of that group. As a political appointee, it's very important to recognize the tremendous power that these bodies have. Secretary ----- spent two years developing a pro-

gram and legislation for creating a ------. It never had a prayer, because he didn't have that coordinating group with him and he had the wrong senator on the committee with the legislation..."

Never believe anything is over and done with.

You may think you've nailed something, lined up all the generals and most of the troops, negotiated a skillful compromise and gotten everyone to sign on. But circumstances and opinions change. When they do--and often even if they don't--you'll find yourself back in the middle of it.

"[The Secretary of State] said something the other day about having to understand that in this city, issues never close. I assume a guy coming out of some traditional industrial organization is used to decisions being made and ending, and going to the next one. Here, it never ends. You think it's finished, but it comes back--it comes in the side door, it comes in the back door."

Develop a network.

"...Every department has a secondary or tertiary link, where subordinates talk to their counterparts. That's very important, because [in government] you have to depend on other people to get things done."

Therefore you have to be certain that some of the people around you can function on this intra-government network.

"You can't wait three months to have people [on your staff whom others can talk to] knowing the message will get through to you."

There's much more message delivery in the way the federal government operates than elsewhere. In a corporate environment, for instance, equals can often communicate frankly and directly. Very little of that occurs between equals in government, except perhaps within the same office. Between offices--say, between an assistant secretary's office and that of the secretary, or the general counsel, or a legislator on the Hill--communication between equals in those offices is much less likely.

"You've got to be much more alert to what the messages mean...because you can't get anything done by yourself. And you've got to have a mechanism to send messages."

"You've got to keep in contact with your counterparts in other departments. You're going to have to deal with a lot of peers."

Control your in-box; don't let it control you.

"Everything's prepared for the top guy...You'd better get ahold of that stuff and delegate it down...Unlike the private sector, where a lot of people will take responsibility, things will be bucked up and no one will take responsibility."

It's a familiar trap. New appointees with just-conferred signature authority spend too much time signing papers and moving them around. That means they're not doing what they should be doing--providing leadership and guidance. Get away from your desk and out of your office frequently. Adopt a hands-on approach.

"It's very easy to get locked at your desk for 24 hours a day and never get through your work pile. And yet you're not brought in to remove things from the in-box to the out-box..."

Not recommended for everybody, however, is the way one young manager solved the problem:

"My in-box grew. Every day I came in there were three in-boxes, and then there were four in-boxes, and so on. So I used to just leave them, and if something was important enough, somebody would eventually come into my office and say something like, 'Did you get that memo I sent you several months ago? It was real important. We ought to get on that'. And we would."

Focus on the difference between thought and action.

"In my view, the easiest part...is coming up with the right answer. The toughest part is getting a large number of people in a department or agency committed to that and to...implementing it."

But both parts are equally vital. Don't emphasize policy making at the expense of management, or vice versa.

"Everyone thinks about taking a job in Washington at a fairly senior level as having to make a choice between 'I'm going to really improve the efficiency of operations' or 'I'm going to take a policy strategy and make my mark.' I think there's a real risk in going to either end of the extreme... You ought to be somewhere in the middle of the continuum..."

Don't think policy making is the exclusive province of political appointees.

"There is this mythology of the policy maker: That up there is someone who is making policy and transmitting down to the troops. In fact, a lot of policy making is started upward and then is decided, and comes back down. My experience was that the career [staff] was absolutely crucial for helping frame and develop policy decisions. Not making them, but setting up any kind of real opportunity to make them... The secretary or the president on their own initiative rarely knew or would anticipate the policy decisions they had to make."

Maintain your perspective.

"If you develop a reputation as a tough son of a bitch, you can always ease up on it. But if you develop a reputation for being had, then you can't walk away from it."

Stay in touch with a wide variety of people on the outside. They don't all have to be closely related to what you're doing, but they should be individuals whose judgment you trust.

"One of the things I made sure I did--as a management tool. I had to keep a perspective on what

> was really going on out there...I used to keep a lot
> of contacts, private sector contacts, and I would
> call them up...and sit around, have a couple of
> beers...and I would ask them: 'How do you feel
> about that?'"

Try to make a distinction between fair-weather friends and the real kind. Don't make any decisions before you're ready to.

> "If you're going into a key position where you have
> some authority over funding or direction, you're
> going to have more friends than you can
> count...They always have the solution to every
> problem you ever thought of. The best thing to do
> is listen and not make any promises."

It is undoubtedly satisfying to achieve something, either personally or collectively. Don't let it go to your head.

> "You go home and still have to take out the
> garbage. You have to realize that it's going to end
> at some point so that when you leave you're not
> destroyed."

Develop a thick skin.

> "No matter what size organization you work in [in
> the private sector], it's very unusual for it to come
> to your attention that a substantial number of
> people think you're a fool and an incompetent. In
> the government, any time you open the newspaper
> you'll find any number of people who say you're a
> fool and incompetent, or dishonest...Most people
> aren't used to that kind of examination."

Nor are most people aware of the subtle impact of this kind of thing on the jobs they are doing in government.

> "It turns out you find yourself reacting to what you
> see in the press, what others say about you, and it
> distorts your priorities. [It] tends to make you
> respond in personal terms and to set your priorities
> in a way that will make you look better but that
> frequently has very little to do with what is best for
> the president..."

To avoid this, some of the following philosophy may help:

> "To the extent that you can, try to understand that the personal attacks on you, your judgment and your honesty that are made in the press and on the cocktail circuit are really reflections only of the major policy and political issues you're involved in, and not something to be taken personally..."

III

YOUR FIRST 90 DAYS

Chapter Summary

Don't try to do it all.

Set three or four priorities for yourself.

Find out early what the problems are...

...attack them quickly...

...but don't be stampeded into unnecessary actions.

Don't try to reorganize everything.

Recognize what you don't know.

Make your own decisions.

Get your timing right.

Throw the general briefing books away.

Figure out ways to get things done.

Don't be afraid to use existing mechanisms.

Make sure people know what's important, which direction you're marching in--and why.

Know what your boss wants.

Never yield to the impulse to go public before you thoroughly understand the issue or problem at hand.

Don't blame predecessors for your current problems.

This is crunch time. No matter how well you've prepared for it, the first weeks are crucial. It is then that you'll make and get your first impressions, learn your way around people, projects and programs, find out what the everyday routines are, make some basic decisions about goals, and set some basic work patterns. While the suggestions that follow apply throughout your time in the job, they're especially important right at the beginning.

Don't try to do it all.

Of the many pieces of wisdom to pass on to those at or near the top of the government, that may be the granddaddy of them all.

> "You're swept up in the glory of power, you have a secretary who gives you a little card that tells you [your schedule each day]. You come to think of yourself as the most important person...and get all charged up to make all these decisions."

Don't try to change that illusory momentum into reality. It's easy to fool yourself, especially at the beginning, into thinking that you can and should tackle the whole agenda.

> "The person who decides he's going to cure all the problems in his agency in two or three years is going to be so diluted and diverted that when he leaves, it won't look a bit different than the day he arrived..."

Set three or four priorities for yourself.

> "Look at the portfolio of the office, its mission, what's been done, what's been undone, what has to be redone. And then make up your mind as to what you can get done."

> "...you have to set aside a certain portion of your

> time to look at the big picture and try to organize
> it so you can provide a leadership role..."

Wisdom, in fact, may lie in making few decisions at all on priorities for awhile.

> "All [of it] should be held for the first 90 days, and
> you should make your own agenda and set your
> own calendar. If those decisions haven't been
> made in the last 90 days they [don't need] to be
> made in the next 90."

Find out early what the problems are...

> "[They include] demands from the external environ-
> ment, often unanticipated, internal pressures--
> inevitable competition for scarce resources, the
> desire of people to have their own particular
> programs move forward. There are noisy constitu-
> encies that have to be satisifed, or silenced, or
> pacified for awhile..."

Learning about the particular problems associated with your job is an important part of the task of setting priorities. Many of the tasks and problems you tackle first are the ones you find waiting for you; like it or not, they go onto your priority list.

> "When you come in and ask what the problems are,
> you first get the bland list, the wish list. Eventu-
> ally, if you persevere, you get the real list, which is
> what are the things you've got to confront. What
> are the things facing the administration that simply
> must be acted on in the next 30 days--regulations,
> programs, etc.?   What are the issues--budget,
> personnel--they must act on in the next 90?"

...attack them quickly...

> "The organization expects you to do that. They
> don't expect you to let problems lie around without
> attention. By that process you show the organiza-
> tion an awful lot about you, much beyond what you
> could ever do in a staff meeting or with a memo.
> In addition, you learn more about the people and

the organization..."

...but don't be stampeded into unnecessary actions.

> "Within a few days of your swearing-in you will
> have on your desk matters which [your staff] says
> you can not duck. They may be regulations, or
> appointments, court-ordered implementation plans,
> or responses to Congressional inquiries. Some of
> these you really have to decide right away. But
> others are things you could let go and don't have
> to decide [right away]. You need to take a careful
> look at those issues before you decide to handle
> them during that crisis time before you really have
> control..."

Many of the routine actions that you are responsible for have been, can be, and should be handled by your staff--under your careful oversight. Don't disturb that process except after due consideration, and then only with restraint.

> "...make sure that 85% of your responsibilities are
> at least running, so that you can crisis manage. It's
> the 15% that's out of whack that you spend most
> of your time on."

Controlling your in-box, discussed earlier, is part of this philosophy. Adopting it will help you to determine where your real priorities lie. That, in turn, is a natural early step in setting or fine-tuning your goals and the strategy for dealing with those goals. Your longer-range priorities are thus likely to be very different from the immediate ones.

Don't try to reorganize everything.

Especially concerning the people and organizations themselves, go slowly.

> "If anyone rolls into a new organization and moves
> too fast, even with the right answers, they'll often
> crash on the shores. The organization that is there
> typically has a lot to offer, and the new people
> should listen to it...People and organizations expect
> to be heard, to be measured, to be considered.
> When you're working a problem, it doesn't take a

long time to [recognize] a mistake, because the
dynamics provide almost instant feedback and you
can make the corrections; the probability of really
messing up is low. But with organizations and
people, you're dealing with things that have long
time constants. If you make a mistake, it takes a
long time to find it out. And that's why...listening
extensively and constantly reassessing the things
you learn are the key ingredients."

Occasionally a big reorganization will be worthwhile on paper. Even
then, the chances are that it is unachievable in fact.

"We had a situation where OMB was all over us,
trying to cut down on the numbers of people in the
agency....I spent a year and a half trying to convince
all the constituencies that a reorganization was the
most efficient way to handle it. I got it to the
President's desk over lots of objections--but then
we left office and it just never went anyplace. It
was a good concept and...it made all the sense in
the world, but it took so much energy and time it
just wasn't worth it. We could have done something else."

Recognize what you don't know.

If you have a major issue or project, look at its history, if any. Find
out what policies have been effective and what the mistakes have been.

"I found that laying out the cons as well as the pros
was something not done very well [for new ap-
pointees]."

"One of the things to ask is why are we doing what
we're doing, and what should we be doing differ-
ently?"

There are various ways to supplement the information and views
available in your office and from your staff:

"When you're in the government, you have no time
to read. And there are all kinds of people outside
who are reading and writing, but it's hard to get it
into your hands in a way that's succinct...One of the
ways is to have a special assistant who goes through

those things. Or you can have a group of people
outside the government that you meet with month-
ly, off the record, to talk about problems, to give
you an alternative to what the staff comes up with."

Make your own decisions.

In the process of recognizing what you don't know, you must also
understand that in some important ways you are building a structure
without detailed blueprints. Being too cautious is a mistake, and allows
others to blaze the trails and set the patterns you'll then have to follow.
You could waste a lot of time waiting for enlightenment that never
comes, for someone to give you information that doesn't exist.

"There's usually relatively little agreement as to
what the goals are that the public-sector manager
is being sent to a Cabinet department or an agency
to carry out. Usually, in a business organization
there's a lot of thought given to exactly what the
goals are, where the organization is in its state of
development; there's always the famous bottom line
to maintain some discipline. But usually there's
also a good understanding of the strategy and what
the company's all about. In the case of many of
the public sector agencies, there may be a broad
general desire to move in a particular direction.
But how you operationalize those goals is usually
something that's very fuzzy..."

Some boldness and risk taking is therefore definitely in order--as long
as you're smart about it.

"There isn't going to be a clear road map. Every
administration is different and you have to figure
out things for yourself..."

It will probably be clear to you that some of the programs and activities you are asked or told to move on would be unwise. This is especially
true when an administration is still finding its way. It means that you
have an educating job to do at the White House or with the secretary
because they simply aren't completely informed about the scene you
inhabit. This is another reason to have the courage of your convictions.

"You will fail if you're too risk-averse...and don't
have some credible positions that you stand up for,
become identified with, and fight with people

about...It's good to say 'keep your head down and learn, etc.' but at some point if you're going to be successful in a very demanding and tough job, you're going to have to stand up for something. You're going to have to get bloody. The time comes when it's better to stand up and maybe fail, and leave a legacy for your successor. You can't be totally defensive and careful and please all the people all the time."

Get your timing right.

You're coming in armed with your own understanding of your administration's policies and programs. You're going to make a careful study of the present organizational set-up and the problems, and identify your priorities, goals and strategy, and the changes you feel are genuinely necessary. When those tasks are accomplished, you're ready to move. But understanding the value of restraint in the changes you make doesn't mean tying yourself inflexibly to what has gone on before you arrive.

"You shouldn't move too fast. But there is a window of time, after you've absorbed all this information and done your homework, when the organization you are running is ready to move. And you should act on that. When you're ready, move aggressively. The people expect it; the constituencies expect it; and you're still in kind of a honeymoon period. If you wait a year or a year and a half, you may have become just sort of the steward for the program. You're sitting at a desk, you're coming to work in the morning, but the place is pretty much running as it always has. If you really want to make some changes, you really have to exercise that window."

"When there's a change of people, there's an opportunity to come in and say 'I've reviewed the policies of the past administration and I really believe that on the whole they did an excellent job, but---.' Then you lay down your list of things you're going to change. That's how progress gets made. You don't defend the Ten Commandments for the rest of your and everybody else's life."

Throw the general briefing books away.

"If possible, ask in advance that none be developed...Choose the issues that you want to know about and ask for briefings on them from specific offices and from individuals. You stand a far greater chance of finding out what you want to know...If you don't say anything at all about briefing books, when you arrive there will be a pile stretching to the ceiling waiting for you. Some of them may even be a little dusty from the last transition and precious few will tell you anything you really want to know about the problems you face."

"Although there is some value to having a book like that on the shelf, what is more useful is something like an executive summary that highlights and crystallizes things..."

Figure out ways to get things done.

"Find the power levers very early, and who controls them. A successful [new appointee] knows where the levers are--how to cut off spending by a given program, how to reallocate resources in the budget, how to make decisions about what people are hired, how far to let your subordinates go in making policy in their areas."

"The first thing you have to do is figure out how to co-opt all the housekeeping functions--the budget process, the personnel, who the constituency groups are...You've got to spend the first four to six months doing all of that..."

"...One of the important things, too, as far as conserving your time goes: You've got to have your short list of people you'll take phone calls from."

Don't be afraid to use existing mechanisms.

> "[Some incoming people] are concerned about
> using a system that's in place--a policy control
> system, a budget system, a planning system. These
> may have been put there by a [predecessor], but
> you can tailor them, make them respond to your
> own particular use. If you throw them out, it will
> be months before there's a new system in place,
> and you will lose time. In fact, while you use them,
> you gain an opportunity to learn how the depart-
> ment runs and how people...do things for you."

Make sure people know what's important, which direction you're marching in--and why.

Simply pushing a button to get something done doesn't work any better in government than in the private sector. If anything, it's worse.

> "I've seen a program where the secretary had
> signed off on something--he wanted it immediately
> --and it was an emergency program that had to go
> into effect in about three weeks to be effective. By
> the time we got cleared by all the various layers,
> even though the secretary's office was screaming
> every day, it was the end of the summer..."

The reasons for these situations are many. Sometimes it's because people forget which part of an agency delivers the actual product:

> "When you think about it, government agencies are
> essentially service operations. At the operating
> level, they provide things to clients just like a bank
> or an insurance agency. If you're always dealing up,
> and not down, your service goes to hell."

You can't of course do your job without "dealing up"--concerning yourself with decision making and decision makers at higher levels. Excessive attention to this, or fascination with it, when the action should be in the other direction can result from confusion between program and policy:

> "In program, the output is down through the
> organization and out. You organize, delegate, and
> it goes--you motivate...Policy is entirely different.

> You can sever yourself entirely from the operations
> and you're effective based on how you deal up."

Sometimes people and agencies dodder and bumble instead of acting because their perceptions fail. They can't separate important matters and the need to be perceptive and inventive about them from the sheer mountain of routine that confronts them:

> "The critical problem in risk-taking in government
> is sorting out what really matters, what is worth
> taking a risk on. It's not just taking a risk for the
> sake of visibility. It's studying and understanding
> issues and deciding whether a very different ap-
> proach is necessary to get out of the very structured
> environment in which you find yourself."

Know what your boss wants.

> "Remember, you're working for somebody. You
> are there to carry out somebody else's agenda.
> That doesn't mean you don't have a role in formu-
> lating that agenda. But you can't go and do
> whatever you want."

> "If you don't know the job you're supposed to be
> performing according to your boss's perspective,
> you've got a problem."

Never yield to the impulse to go public before you thoroughly understand the issue or problem at hand.

This is vitally important in the early months.

> "It's so tempting to go ahead and get out front,
> especially if you're getting pressure from the White
> House or wherever to announce some new policy
> position, to make some news. It's very tough to
> resist those pressures, but it's essential."

> "The first thing that happens when somebody gets
> appointed is that they want them on *Face the Nation*
> or a quote for the *Washington Post,* or whatever. And
> people don't want to seem like total dummies, so they
> sometimes make commitments and statements that

later they wish they hadn't made because they can't
live up to them..."

Don't blame predecessors for your current problems.

"It's not very graceful. And they're all going to be
blamed on you anyway."

IV

THE CAREER SERVICE

Chapter Summary

Rid yourself of preconceptions about the career service.

Learn from the professionals.

Find out who can get the job done.

Mold your staff carefully.

Recognize the importance of credibility and respect.

Communicate well and regularly.

Involve the career staff.

Build esprit and morale.

Don't reorganize for personnel reasons.

Two million people work for the federal government. Another two million serve the armed forces in uniform. Most of them are professional government employees. For them, government is work, career, life.

An unwritten rule of conduct enjoins them, as objective professionals, to provide quality service to all administrations, regardless of the party in power or their personal political beliefs.

> "People were remarkably loyal. If they were enlisted in the process, they were surprisingly willing to follow policy I'm sure they didn't agree with. I find that to be an innate characteristic of the [career] service--the degree of non-ideological response."

Look at the federal career service (not "the bureaucracy") and you'll see certain features that are identical with those of any other group of employees. There are the high achievers, full of energy, ambition, imagination and promise; the drones holding down desks or waiting to retire; and the majority ranged along the spectrum in between.

But in other respects, career servants march to a different drummer. Their hiring, salaries, promotions, health care, working hours, vacations, retirement, and much else besides are clocked by regulations that are generally standard across the government. Upper-level career salaries-- those of the Senior Executive and Senior Foreign Services--are tied to the salary levels of members of Congress. And where else would you find such lengthy procedures for hiring, such formidable barriers to firing, and such exasperating obstacles even to moving employees to other jobs or locations?

For the senior political appointee, there are two fundamental "don'ts" where career people are concerned. First, don't underestimate them--a mistake common to newcomers. Many career professionals are terrifical- ly good at what they do. Second, avoid any notion that you can somehow run your job without them. You can't.

> "Political appointees tend to believe that they can manage only through the handful of people who come in with them. You'll kill yourself if you do that."

No question, you're the boss of your particular domain. It should never be otherwise. But some careerists function in command positions in their own right, and with good reason. Quite a few others have the experience and talent to do so.

You'll be in the job for two, three, four years. That may seem a short time, compared to where you've been or are going next. Developing productive relationships with career staff may not rank high on your list of what you want to do and where you want to go. Yet, with with all its good and bad features, that same staff will be key in helping you get there.

Work closely with your staff, run it firmly, and get from it all the help you can.

Rid yourself of preconceptions about the career service.

Instead, base your judgments on what you see as you go along.

> I went to Washington with a very low regard for the bureaucrat...but came away with a much higher regard..."

> "Many career people are competent, experienced, ready to be helpful. Locate and identify the best of these early in your tenure, without regard for political affiliation or inclination."

Most appointees will have to manage staffs and budgets larger than they are used to. As we've seen, wise use of the career staff will free you to perceive the handful of projects and programs you are most interested in and have the ability to affect.

> "Let the career people run most of the rest, keeping you informed."

> "What you discover...is that [they] can keep things going. I was there for about two weeks when [a former President] died. So [the White House chief of staff] calls me up and says 'You're in charge of the funeral.' What the hell do I do? An hour later some colonel showed up with a book that thick. What I was going to do for -----'s funeral had been written up for years...All the stuff was done. We

had parades. We had horses. We had brass bands. So until you find that colonel, you are in deep trouble."

George Bush's view of the career service, after years in public life at high levels of the federal government, is reflected in this comment just days after he became President:

> "...I have not known a finer group of people than those I have worked with in government."

Learn from the professionals.

> "...they are the repository of institutional knowledge and experience that cannot possibly be duplicated by some assistant secretary, even if he or she is the savviest politician in the world."

> "Long-term career people can point out for a political appointee where a lot of land mines are, politically; who's interested in that subject on the Hill; who you're going to have trouble with. There's a lot of political intelligence that builds up in the career staff."

As you work into the job, and if your staff gets the right vibes from you, that kind of intelligence will begin to flow to you naturally. But at first, mining it may be hard.

> "There is almost always [at least] one person...who's been around for a long time, knows all the bodies ...If you can find that man or woman and befriend them and get them to give you the real kind of inside skinny on what's going on, that's very helpful. You've got to find the intelligence network inside the system."

Find out who can get the job done.

> "You have to rely on the professionals. And the real issue there [is] finding out whom [you can] rely on, which you do by independent judgment--by giving them assignments to see what comes back... There are people there who are top professionals...

> "Although your peers may be political and have a sense of where you're coming from and what you're trying to get done, 98 percent of the [career staff] don't have any idea what that is. Getting that across to people, finding out who you can trust, testing them to find out who you can rely on--I think that is just vital."

> "...I don't mean whom I can trust politically, but who is going to give me a straight report on the state of affairs around the swirling policy issues that I'm going to be called to act on..."

The same principle applies here as in early decision making: Play it cool; don't be in a hurry.

> "It's important not only to reserve judgment in the first 90 days about what those various senior professionals are coming at you with, in terms of their agendas, but also to sort out who's really going to reinforce your own two or three objectives..."

In assessing your staff, also keep in mind what a former appointee calls the "time frame concept:"

> "The person committed to a career is looking at things in a different way than the person who comes in with a typical two-year stint. It becomes very important to be able to distinguish between the person who is reading you for his or her own interest--who may be very good at sensing what it is [you] want and responding to that whether it's right or wrong--versus the person you can really count on to help you, who's going to give you independent judgment, going to tell you when you're wrong, going to provide that kind of balance."

Mold your staff carefully.

You want cohesion, productivity and balance, not only in your personal staff but among the larger group of people working under your authority. In building such a group, a little self-knowledge is valuable.

> "You've got to analyze your strengths and weak-
> nesses and [make use of] people who will comple-
> ment you. You've got to be cognizant of that, right
> from the beginning."

When it comes to shaping your personal staff, give as much attention to support as to substantive people. Both kinds are vital, and they need to work smoothly together in good times and bad. Choose them thoughtfully.

> "Look carefully at that administrative assistant...If
> she has survived through a couple of administra-
> tions she must have something good going for her.
> Consider keeping her on."

If you have special assistants, give them specific assignments or roles and make sure they understand and stay within them. A special assistant who breaks away into open-field running will undermine the authority and effectiveness of the boss.

> "They [should be] your link to the staff, not free
> wheelers...It's better to find someone who has pre-
> established relationships than to bring in a stranger.
> You need eyes, ears, nose--but you don't need a
> mouth."

Work hard to merge your career and appointed people into a seamless group who operate together effectively.

> "The keystone to effective government is an
> immediate commitment, from the day you walk in,
> to forcing a marriage between career [staff] and
> political appointees..."

Not every senior appointment carries with it the authority to bring in staff from the outside. If you have that authority and want to take advantage of it, use restraint.

> "Bring in too many...and they'll be tripping over
> themselves and you. Bring in only enough to
> provide an impetus to change, so that you can feel
> you have control..."

> "You have to be careful not only about who you
> bring in with you, but whether you bring many at
> all or try to make use of who's there. My general
> practice was [to try] not to bring anyone with

> me...Take one or two of the top career people and
> bring them up; make them some of your key
> assistants."

Many feel, however, that--if the situation permits--certain assistance
brought in from outside is highly useful.

> "Bring in somebody with you that you trust, and
> knows you and your management methods. That
> is just critical. I don't care what agency it is. Once
> you're there, you're not going to be seeing the light
> of day for 90 days."

Recognize the importance of credibility and respect.

The point itself hardly needs demonstrating. But, just for the record:

> "...you'll never get there without winning the
> confidence of the career people. It's one of the
> publics you have to bring along, and it's probably
> the first one. If you don't convince the career staff
> that you are a competent leader, that you know
> what you want, and that you'll bring them along,
> then you're going to be in trouble everywhere else."

As elsewhere in life, first impressions in government are generally the
deepest. They are also the hardest to dislodge.

> "Whether you're an appointee or a career employ-
> ee, the natural tendency [is for each to think] that
> the other is bad. You have to recognize that
> assumption is the beginning of the relationship.
> Usually, at the end of an education period where
> you get to know each other, that distinction goes
> away. The problem for the new guy coming in is:
> How do you reduce that length of time before trust
> develops? I think more people ought to focus on
> that, because most of the time it starts off as war
> and that's the wrong way to start."

To be sure, some former appointees are skeptical about too much
reliance on trust and respect, and warn against being taken over by the
career staff. They refer to the opportunities some career people sometimes have--if they choose to take it--to influence an appointee's decisions
and actions in directions they prefer, or even arrange that events conspire
to thwart or embarrass a boss they don't like. As one appointee ex-
pressed it, the career staff "can make you or break you." The best advice

on this point seems to lie somewhere in the middle:

> "There's a concern about being captured by your
> own people, which I think is legitimate because
> they're naturally interested [in their own] ends--
> they want more funding, or there's a certain
> amount of empire building. And I'm not saying
> that's wrong. It's just sort of a natural thing. But
> if you have those two concerns too much on your
> shoulders and worry about the trust aspect or
> about being captured, you'll never have anybody
> supporting you to do anything..."

One way to help defuse the entire issue ahead of time is to make it clear that you know trust is a two-way street.

> "People come into Washington with an attitude of
> either giving or taking. The rank and file will spot
> it right away when someone is an exploiter, just
> wants to come in and hold the job and take
> whatever..."

Avoid the mistake of going into the job expressing doubt about the individual or collective political loyalty of career staff. Clearly, some of them will be less enthusiastic than others about a given administration's political philosophy. But all have a right to their own private views. At the same time, as careerists they understand the principles and traditions of their profession. To question loyalty publicly is destructive both of staff morale and support, and of your chances of getting anything done.

> "Secretary ----- never outlived his remarks to us at
> lunchtime...He brought the whole State Department
> staff together--which in those days was not that
> big--and he got up and said 'I want you to know
> that all these stories about disloyalty in the State
> Department I recognize are untrue. I know full
> well that *most* of you are loyal.' He never recov-
> ered from that..."

The importance of credibility in turn re-emphasizes the urgent need, discussed earlier, that positions like yours be filled with people whose experience and training--competence, in a word--equips them to perform well. If you are mismatched with your job, leadership of your staff will come very hard indeed:

> "If you're going to have credibility with the civil
> service staff, you'd better bring your credentials

with you. If you don't have credentials before you get there, it's harder than hell to build them once you are..."

Communicate well and regularly.

"Have open communications with the people in your office and you'll find that most of the time they'll follow you pretty much where you want to go."

The need for good communication with your staff is clear enough, and not very different from that in any private sector organization. Because government is a bigger and more dispersed enterprise with more individuals involved, however, this need takes on added urgency. First, you have to get your staff intellectually and viscerally involved in what you're trying to do.

"Let people know what you're trying to accomplish and make them feel they can associate with [it]."

Second, use communication as a management tool to aid the carrying out of assignments and the handling of vast amounts of work that you don't see. One of the many small and routine ways to do this is to be sure your people get copies of every speech you make.

"You have to teach the people who report to you the values you are trying to implement in the context of the program. That's for two reasons. One, so that they understand you when you tell them to do something. Two, for those thousands of things that never get to you, you're teaching them how to think about them and how to react to them."

It's a principle that works at any level of government, but especially at and near the top:

"President Johnson used to invite us over to the White House and give us lectures. The lectures were in Texas analogies, of course. What he was trying to do was explain to us his value system that we would apply to contingencies, programs and questions that never got near the White House. I was very impressed with that."

A recent Cabinet secretary was admired in many quarters for his efficient and likeable leadership style. He used to cite three simple rules for communicating with his employees.

> "Be specific about what you want to do. State the end result that you expect. State when you want it completed."

In communicating, don't rely exclusively on the chain of command. Go down into the organization and rub shoulders.

> "One of the things I did when I was in the Secretary of -----'s office was to go down inside the Bureau of ------, for example, and talk to the people who generated the individual line items... And I said 'Now just tell me how this works.' Well, the image everybody had was that you could never find out. But what I found was that this was the first time somebody from the Secretary's office had ever been there--and they'd pull out their lower left-hand drawer and show me..."

To put it another way:

> "[There is] not enough communication with the ultimate doer of a given task. You can cope with this through innovative management. Have one-on-one contact or access, not a long line of people to get policies implemented through."

Involve the career staff.

> "...there's absolutely no reason not to involve [them] ...If you approach it with that kind of attitude, you minimize the likelihood that it will become a 'we-they' type of system. Instead, it becomes the office together."

This is also a case where the benefits flow in both directions.

> "You need people in the Senior Executive Service or even lower whom you can bring in, have meetings with, and elicit their ideas...sort of make your issues their issues. It gives them a little pride of authorship, a vested interest..."

Build esprit and morale.

> "People work in government for essentially unsel-
> fish reasons. They have a spirit of public service
> and are motivated by it. I found it important to
> show [my employees] that I understood that."

Here again, first impressions are important.

> "When you go into an organization you've got to
> understand that you are not some kind of hatchet
> person, that you are not there to clean house...Your
> job is to go in there and let those people know that
> you know they are professionals."

And, with that point very clear, lose no time in treating them like
professionals. Give them every reason to do their best, to excel, to be
creative. It's a good way to discover where the talent and energy is.
When they respond, or when they try to, find ways to recognize it.

> "Encourage people to take risks--and reward them
> whether those risks are successful or not...Coming
> up with new ideas, new ways of doing things, and
> testing them out. I think, increasingly, that people
> who are willing to [take risks] are not encouraged,
> not rewarded. I find the people who are promoted
> are the 'go-alongs.'"

Under the pressure of your responsibilities, it's all too easy to push
staff considerations to the back of your mind. If this happens repeatedly,
trouble is just around the corner.

> "My tendency was to get totally caught up in the
> issues. The White House is on your back, OMB is
> on your back, the Congress is on your back, you're
> always making public appearances, and you forget
> totally that you've got a couple of thousand people
> working for you who have the same kinds of
> needs...You'd never ignore that kind of thing in
> business, but often businessmen who go into
> government get caught up with the whole policy
> aspect and forget about the organization."

You need the career staff to be there for you. They need the same--
and fully understand what your schedule and time constraints are. But
you have to give your staff as much careful attention as you can make
room for. In this, even mere perceptions of your attitude can help.

"I would look for as many opportunities as possible to build the morale of the employees through various techniques which really don't cost that much--meeting with the senior managers, [giving people] opportunities to make presentations to the assistant secretary or the secretary, talking to them about what they do. That goes a long way..."

What you want to avoid at any cost is creating a wasteland where your staff writes you off as a "taker" and just waits you out. As a onetime appointee describes that situation:

"They look at you like a kidney stone: 'You, too, shall pass.'"

Don't reorganize for personnel reasons.

On arriving in the job, you may find in place one or more career people who don't please you, or seem unsuitable to your plans. You may think that reorganizing the office is the way to deal with it. But a wide majority of former appointees advises against it. It's better to take on the often trying procedures required to move an individual out, than to shake up the entire structure.

"The organization will respond positively if you confront personnel issues correctly. It turns out that, if there's somebody who isn't pulling his or her own weight, [other people in the same organization have] known it for a long time. Rather than reorganizing around that person, you can move them out of the job without adding three extra boxes to the chart. It will generate enormous good will in the organization."

V

THE CONGRESS

Chapter Summary

Begin your relationship with the Congress even before your confirmation hearing.

Get to know the members important to your work.

Develop relationships with committee and members' personal staff.

Know how the system operates, and what your members are interested in.

Learn the ropes of Congressional testimony.

Never forget that members of Congress are primarily responsible to constituents.

"Before my formal confirmation hearing, I was one of several nominees called to talk to members of the Committee privately. When my turn came I went in, and there was some back-and-forth around the table between them and me, the usual thing. I thought it was about over when Senator ---- came in. He plowed around in my record awhile and then looked at me and said, 'Now, I'd like to ask you about this vicious eight-page attack on the Congress of the United States that you authored and was reported in ------'s column. What do you have to say about that?' I said, 'Senator, I haven't the slightest idea what you're talking about'. And then one of his staff leaned over to him and whispered, 'Senator, it's not this guy, it's the *next* one!'"

That story particularly amuses experienced government people because it is a reminder that even the best-prepared, best-briefed legislator can make mistakes. But, unlike the happy outcome in this case, you can't count on avoiding Congressional ire, even when it's misplaced.

There are certain things, however, that you can absolutely rely on from the Congress. Close attention to what you're up to. Phone calls from staffers and letters from Members, asking for information, applying pressure--or both. Summonses to testify in committee. Requests for favors or help for individual constituents.

The Congress, like other power centers in a city of plural points of responsibility, will have a lot to say about what you do, how you do it, and whether you succeed. Yet, if you talk to a random selection of executive branch colleagues about the Hill, you're likely to find only a minority who feel they truly understand how the place works.

"The average person who comes from industry hasn't a clue what dealing with Congress means. When you're in an administration with a short time fuse, your number one objective is to get something done. Congress's number one objective is to get re-elected..."

That thumbnail view is clearly onesided. But it expresses the kind of short-tempered frustration that exposure to the Congress can generate. For the legislative branch is a singularly complex institution--immensely powerful, labyrinthine in conducting its business, self-contradictory, self-protective to a fault. Its recent critics, within the Congress and outside, have given it mediocre marks on a number of counts. They have under-scored what they see as its leisurely work pace and low productivity; its more maddening rules of procedure; its vulnerability to exterior sources of influence and income; even the increasingly disturbing fact, on the House side, that incumbents are being re-elected in overwhelming majorities.

Happily, the current leadership seems to be moving in the direction of correcting some of these situations more determinedly than at any time in recent memory. In this, they are propelled by the clear desire of many members that constitutes one of the strongest impulses to internal reform since World War II.

Their success, if it comes, will probably make co-existence with the Congress easier in some ways for the other branches of government. But it won't alter the everlasting need for executive branch seniors to learn their way around the Hill, know the members and staff who matter to their agencies and jobs, and do business with them effectively.

Begin your relationship with the Congress even before your confirmation hearing.

> "If your position is subject to confirmation, make your courtesy calls, make them early, and make them on both sides of the aisle. Everybody's important."

Adopt this rule from the beginning: Don't wait for the Congress to call you. Whatever business you have with the Hill, be the initiator.

Plan, schedule and carry out *all* your calls in careful coordination with the Congressional liaison office of your agency; seek their advice and listen to it.

> "...you can...learn a lot immediately from the legislative and press guys (Congressional liaison and public affairs officers of an agency). [They] are invaluable guides. You're not going to like what you hear, but you've got to believe it..."

Get to know the members important to your work.

These, of course, are the people you'll call on first, and obviously the key individuals are the chairs and ranking minority members of each committee, in both Houses, that will have oversight or jurisdiction in whole or in part over your agency's work in general, and your job in particular.

> "There are a lot of Presidential appointees that come to town and forget they were appointed by the President but confirmed by the Congress. I've sat with more people who didn't understand that those committee chairmen, particularly in the House, are damned important to what they're trying to do."

After that come other members of those committees, of both parties. If your level of responsibilities and position warrant it, consider calling as well on the leadership of both Houses--in both parties.

But there's yet another vital connection to make:

Develop relationships with committee and members' personal staff.

> "Don't deal only or necessarily with the principals. The staff are going to shape everything, especially as the Hill has become more fragmented. Find the staff guy who happens to be the expert in that particular area and work with him. Because he's really running the system. The principals are too busy doing too many [other] things."

> "Don't be caught up in your own importance so much that you won't take a mid-level person from the Hill to lunch. He can really make you or break you early on..."

Creating relationships with staff can sometimes be a delicate matter. You may sense, for example, that contact with a staffer could tread on the toes of a member--or of another staffer. Or maybe, in setting out to establish your contacts with given staff members, you are puzzled about how staff responsibilities are carved up, or how particular members of the staff relate to each other. There are ways to help clear up such questions and avoid potential problems:

> "Ask your committee chairman: 'Who is your key staff person? Whom do you want me to relate to?'"

Know how the system operates, and what your members are interested in.

> "I was incredibly impressed at how good he was. He was successful not because he took the ideas that he thought were right but that he always saw these ideas from the Congressman's point of view. He realized that this guy out there has a problem that's different from mine and if I can help him find a solution--no matter whether he is a Democrat or a Republican--then I can sell this policy which I think is the right policy."

Elaborating on that general theme,

> "You've got to sit down [with the relevant members] and say 'look, can we--not I--do this? What do you want to see done with this agency?' Not 'what do I want to see done?' What you're getting is other people's agendas. And you're finding out whether they can support you. You know your agenda will never fit with theirs a hundred percent."

Finding common ground and trading favors for mutual benefit is a solidly pragmatic approach to the Congress. For their part, you'll find that the legislators have different levels of skill in this regard. But most of them will have had more experience at it than you.

> "Every member of Congress does everything on that basis. Some are better at it than others; some know how to play hardball better than others. But very few political appointees know how to do it."

Always remember that individual members of the Congress, and frequently committees as a whole, move in a many-sided world where numerous interests are at stake. It's a world where achievement is not often a matter of dominating the scene and hammering your objective home, or selling something to the person who makes the key decision. It's much more a case of trading one set of considerations against another, or against several others--of supporting other peoples' agendas in return for support of your own.

> "In the private sector, when you want to sell something, you put together the most rational case you can and you take it to whomever and you try to persuade them. If you do that in the Congress, you may advance two percent of the way. It's the other, overwhelming set of issues which have nothing to do with the case you're trying to sell."

In all of your relationships on the Hill, keep in your mind a picture of how the members see you. However critical your issues and however talented you are in presenting them and arguing your points, remember that members of Congress have seen a lot of people in your position come and go. All the more reason not to expend your efforts in directions where they will do you little good. Know your targets.

> "...there are barons in the Congressional system. There are some people who have a lot of votes in their pockets, and others who have none. Most political appointees totally miss that distinction. They go rushing off thinking they have full support from so-and-so on this, that or the other thing, and of course so-and-so doesn't have that much clout and they don't get any place. You've got to identify who the real peer movers are. Those are the ones to build your personal relationships with."

Learn the ropes of Congressional testimony.

When appearing before a committee, or talking informally to individual members or groups, equip yourself to do the job. To most hearings you'll bring along prepared opening remarks which become part of the record. That's the easy part. Think also about the questions you may get and work out some answers ahead of time.

> "They really want to know whether the principal witness knows what he's talking about. I also learned that, if you don't know the answer, tell them you don't but you'll get it fast. Then get it back to them within 24 hours. That usually buys you some grace time."

Obviously, part of the job of briefing yourself beforehand is reading up to date on the subject at hand and--again--using your relationships with Congressional staff.

"Never go up to a committee without someone on your staff having talked to the staffers."

"We'd actually call people and ask how important this is to the Senator. We'd try to get a feel for it."

"Not one of my...colleagues took the time to get acquainted with the Congressional staffers or to read the files. If you go back and look at the [hearing record] you'll see that they all got beaten up on because they were very frequently surprised by the topics that came up. Unfortunately, given the adversarial situation that had come about, it wasn't a time when you could say you don't know but will find out. They all ended up pretty badly battered..."

You can gear your own office in ways that enhance the quality and effectiveness of your Hill appearances.

"Be sure, in your intimate staff, that you have somebody who comes from the Hill, who comes with strong credentials, in whose judgment you have absolute confidence...Essentially the Congressional relations office in your department works for you. And if they do a good job, then you don't need someone on your staff. If they don't do a good job...then you do need someone...You can educate the Congressional relations office. But you can't afford to fail because they don't do their job right. You don't have that option..."

When possible, avoid testifying as a member of a panel on which opposing objectives or viewpoints are represented. Panels of this kind give committee members an opportunity to play witnesses off against each other.

"If they want you to testify, testify by yourself. You have a right to insist on that. It's important because lots of times they like to throw you on a panel and chew you up alive. Usually they try to set up these panels to sandbag the administration."

Never forget that members of Congress are primarily responsible to their constituents.

"One of the keys to decent relations on Capitol Hill is something that many [appointees] don't have, and that is a genuine respect--I mean a genuine respect--for the role of Congressmen. If you think constantly that they're just there to manipulate, or if you derogate their jobs, if you don't understand how difficult their jobs are, you're never going to be able to deal with them. You [have to understand] that a Congressman is serving his constituents back home, and there are certain things he has to ask and do, that he does have this responsibility as an elected official. You have to have real respect for that, not just a grudging sense of it all."

VI

THE BUDGET

Chapter Summary

Don't make big decisions until you know the ropes of budgeteering.

In preparing a budget, start at the beginning.

Take a common-sense approach to OMB.

Use OMB and the budget process itself to learn.

Learn the strategy and tactics.

Involve career staff in the budget process.

You or your boss or the head of your agency will have very firm ideas about what kind of money it will take to carry out policy and achieve desired goals. So will the Congress and the Office of Management and Budget (the budget and policy enforcer in the President's executive office). It's pretty safe to assume that none of these three sets of ideas will start out in the same ballpark, and maybe not even in the same city.

Each year you'll be involved in a cyclical drama called the budget process. As Act I begins, your agency tells OMB the size and shape of the budget it thinks it needs. At the end, after a lot of dialogue, OMB tells your agency how much it can ask for and the figure becomes part of the President's budget message to the Congress.

In Act II, your agency shapes legislative requests based on the budget message and--in the person of seniors like yourself--takes them to the Hill and asks for the money. When the final curtain drops, the Congress has acted in one form (appropriation) or another (continuing resolution) and your agency gets budget authority and can spend the money.

It's always possible that the final annual figure will bear some resemblance to your agency's original projections. Times, of course, are hard. This is and will continue indefinitely to be the age of austerity in government. Get used to the fact that funding for your programs and activities will almost always be insufficient--not merely to get the best of all possible results, but in many cases just to keep things running.

The budget is a fundamental element of government, and of the lives of those who govern. You are likely to be involved each year in the entire process. You'll help to shape your agency's proposals and contribute to their defense at OMB--a due-process consultation in which agencies can and do take their cases on key issues to very high levels, including the Oval Office. You'll help defend budget legislation on the Hill. Even more to the point, you'll be responsible for seeing that the money made available in your area of responsibility is spent as productively as possible directly along the lines of administration policy. You'll have to be creative in making it stretch as far as possible. In these efforts, you'll normally function under the intense gaze of OMB and the Congress, and be continually accountable to both.

A former appointee correctly calls the budget process "one of the main tools you have to set priorities and one of your primary constraints." In other words, it's a source of grief, but--more important--a highly useful implement.

Don't make big decisions until you know the ropes of budgeteering.

"The discussion that has to go on right away on the budget can be extremely difficult for a new appointee. You're interacting mainly with the budget office and there are all sort of arcane things you have to know about the process, as well as the substance of the proposals. If you can, delay substantive decisions, especially notions of new legislation, temporarily until you get past the first budget cycle."

In preparing a budget, start at the beginning.

"The first step is not to have the budget assistant secretary come in and tell you all about the numbers. The first step is to sit down and figure out your function, what are your policy objectives. Develop the policy intelligently, [based on] the President's philosophy. In the process...you should be touching base both with the previous occupants of the position, your outside constituencies and your inside constituencies. Blend all those together and come up with a position and get it cleared. And then you meet with the budget guy and say, all right, now here are the objectives I want to achieve. What kind of resources do I have and what do I have to go after to get more...Ninety-five percent of the time new appointees go into the process without all of that policy preparation and start driving their policy decisions from the budget point of view. And that's exactly ass backwards."

As you develop policy positions in the budget preparation exercise, talk also to those who are not your constituents.

"You may find that if you just talk to your constituencies, you won't find people who will criticize the
policy direction in which you're going."

One non-constituency to stay in touch with are those elsewhere in the
government who review what you do to see what you're achieving.

"For example, the General Accounting Office
people. [They] look at programs from a somewhat
different perspective than the people who run the
programs inside. And, while you may want to go
with your internal constituencies or even your
external ones, they're a good check. They're a little
more objective."

Take a common-sense approach to OMB.

"Think of the OMB people as though, if you were
in the private sector, they were the stock market
analysts that follow your company. You've got to
convince [them] all the time that management is
good in your company, that stock prices are going
to continue to go up under your management, that
you have respect for their attitude. Give them everything you possibly can in the way of information..."

Recognize that OMB is the President's policy and budget instrument,
one that must often be wielded bluntly. Try, however, to avoid the mind-
set that OMB is the foe.

"If you can persuade these people that you have
the right approach on the policy side --which probably appeals most to the people at OMB, who want
to be policy makers themselves rather than be
considered as bean counters--if you can involve
them early on in the process you're trying to develop and explain what they have in that policy, they'll
be on your side when it comes to addressing the
numbers. From the appointee's perspective you
can't [take the position] that OMB is somehow the
enemy."

Use OMB and the budget process itself to learn.

> "Probably the best and most objective source of information about what goes on in an agency when you come in as a political appointee is the budget person who's been handling [an] agency for awhile. They are very smart, objective career people. They've spent years trying to figure out what makes that institution work. They're happy to share the information they have."

Frequently, an appointee doesn't get all sides of an argument on issues and implementation by listening only to immediate staff--or others in the agency. But the leathery career veterans at OMB, who help to lower the boom on you when necessary, can also be a source of different and useful insights.

> "You're trying to go home about 7:30 at night and someone comes into your office and says your testimony for tomorrow hasn't been cleared by OMB. So another hour goes by before you [talk to OMB] and for the first time you're hearing arguments why what the people who've been telling you what you should do might not be correct. The staff at OMB has a lot of good arguments [which your own staff may not buy]. And you've got to work against that current all the time, and make a good relationship with your counterpart at OMB."

Learn the strategy and tactics.

No matter what kinds of contacts you develop around town on budget matters, you have to understand how the system by which budgets are negotiated works, and make it work for you when possible. A good example is the legitimate use of Congressional power to keep in your budget what you really want to keep.

> "In negotiating your budget with OMB, the big trick is what you give up. You only get four or five issues you can take to the President, so you have to negotiate the whole thing down. It's important to know which ones the Congress [will get] so much pressure on that, even though you agree [with OMB] to leave them out of the budget, [the Con-

gress] will put them back in. When you fight with OMB, these are the giveaways you are going to trade."

Another example is the knowledgeable use of internal executive branch procedures to advance or protect your budget interests.

"One of the tricks is choosing the route--whether something is going to be...part of the [regular] budget process; or of the Cabinet Council process where OMB is just another head at the table as opposed to having complete control..."

What that means is that, in the latter case, budget decisions are more likely to take the form of policy changes carrying little or no direct budgetary impact.

Involve career staff in the budget process.

"...there has been a tendency not to let career directors [of legislative affairs offices of agencies] be involved as directly as I think they have to be with the staffs on the Hill. As long as it's clear that [they] are there to provide information about what's going on with respect to Congressional requests, they can provide a lot of grease...between the Hill and the executive branch which, if it's not done, will result in unnecessary conflict for the administration, no matter who's in...The career people...can legitimately perform very important information-gathering and communication functions."

VII

THE PRESS

Chapter Summary

Recognize that there is a different code for judging behavior in government.

Understand the importance of perception.

Remember that staff are there to help you.

Find out which reporters are important to your agency and your objectives.

Don't wait for the press to discover you. Make the first move.

Understand how to work with the press to gain your objectives.

Don't adopt the easy notion that good news is no news.

Stay abreast of what's in the press--and what's likely to be.

Get a firm grasp on the different ground rules for talking with the press.

Handle interview requests judiciously.

Don't go into an interview cold.

Tell the truth.

Cut your losses.

Whether bad stories are true or false, don't crawl into a hole.

Understand how leaks work--and avoid them when possible.

> "Part of this is being comfortable with yourself and being able to deal with your own ego. If you haven't got it under control, stay out of this town..."

That may be the best single piece of media advice for a political appointee in Washington. If you ignore it, you'll be setting yourself up to walk straight into some of the common traps and pitfalls which can waylay any senior federal executive.

But it's really not hard to enjoy the right kind of press attention in the capital or develop good relationships with journalists. Something like 75% of it is taking an intelligent look at the environment you've been catapulted into, and using your head to navigate it. The rest is learning some technique and a handful of ground rules.

> "The media is so pervasive now that anyone who comes to Washington who does not understand the fundamentals of what's going on with the media in this country, probably shouldn't be in Washington... Obviously, they should watch it very closely, they should take advice from people who understand it and know how it works. If you go to Washington thinking you can do your job despite the press, or working against them, you're wrong. You cannot do it. ...The first question that should [be] asked in [any] decision is, what's the media going to say about it?"

A look, first, at the new landscape and common sense.

Recognize that there is a different code for judging behavior in government.

> "There are standards in Washington that the press looks at that you don't have in the private sector. Things that were perfectly okay [there] are going to be looked on as improper in government, and

> you're going to be embarrassed. Something happens--you took a trip, brought in someone for a consulting job, deducted a vacation. You have to understand the sensitivities of such things in Washington."

Understand the importance of perception.

> "In many cases, it's not a question of whether it gets out, but how...You need to know what you're doing to make sure the message gets out constructively."

> "Sometimes, instead of putting 100% of your effort into the technical quality of what you're doing, settling for 90% and putting the other 10% into promoting it will actually take the program further."

In government no less than other sectors of American society you must reckon with two phenomena. One is the role of image--what something seems, not necessarily what it is. The second, a corollary of the first, is that the marketing of an idea (or a product, or a politician) can be almost as important as the idea itself.

Whatever your personal feelings about the relative values of reality vs. image, never underestimate the importance of intelligent communications, and of perception as a factor in what you are doing.

Remember that staff are there to help you.

> "You've got to create some kind of buffer between yourself and the press so that you can control the situation..."

> "Everything you do has Congressional or media interest at some point along the way. You're going to run into something and you have to know what to do."

Get to know the director of your agency's press and information operation, however small or occasional it may be. Familiarize yourself with what it does and how, how it affects you, how its staff can serve you.

Make it clear that you are interested in working with them, ask how you can be helpful, and give them ready access to you.

Find out which reporters are important to your agency and your objectives.

"There are more than 3,000 reporters living and working in Washington, and they are not equal..."

Not everyone can work for the *New York Times* or a major network. Not everyone wants to. But don't dismiss the majority who don't. Even those who labor for small, or obscure, or specialized trade publications have a job to do, and may make the crucial difference on an issue or story that matters greatly to you. Know as wide a range of journalists as you comfortably can. Develop the habit of asking exactly what they cover and how. Where not already obvious, it can also be useful to find out what if any political philosophy guides their editors and publishers. Most important, know which ones are most reliable for accuracy, fairness, and respect for the ground rules governing your contacts with them.

Don't wait for the press to discover you. Make the first move.

"Periodically I [brought] in the press that covers my area and just [had] coffee and doughnuts with them. Just to give them a chance to know me and figure out who I am, because the beats of these people change. It gives them a feeling you're open, they get a chance to ask questions, and...to know who you are. This gives you a chance to get a fair [hearing] because all [your] constituent groups are after them and want to get their story told."

Develop constructive contacts with individual reporters and keep them that way. Then, when the inevitable problems arise, you have relationships to work with in which each side has some confidence. But don't expect a free ride from reporters, however good your relationships with them are.

Understand how to work with the press to gain your objectives.

They'll certainly want to use you for theirs, so get something in return; it's a two-way street. Calling public attention to a project or an achievement, explaining or emphasizing the value of a particular policy, setting the record straight on a given issue--these and more are legitimate uses of the media. Reporters often don't have to be coaxed into covering such exercises; they have to cover their beats, and need and want to know.

> "Not using them is a mistake. They can be a good resource. You have to learn how. It's important to give the press substance. Learn to give quotes that are quotable. You can have a tremendous influence on what in fact is used if you are careful how you say it."

Only reporters and/or their editors can decide the news value of an event, or how much coverage to give it. Therefore, don't constantly or frantically seek their attention, or lose time fretting if you don't get it. Once you do have it, don't waste it. Be informative, concise, interesting, imaginative, original, funny, honest, and human.

The trade press is frequently more useful than the general media in getting across your policy, comment, or reaction than the general or political press. Because it is specialized, it is apt to be more receptive to you, and can be a precision tool for reaching the people most directly concerned. But don't go this route if the issue at hand transcends that special audience, and what you want to convey needs a wider hearing.

Don't adopt the easy notion that good news is no news.

> "The press is out to get headlines, sell newspapers. Good news doesn't do that. So they won't go where there is good news; they go where there's bad news."

Well, not really. But people, especially people in government, start believing this old absurdity after a while and saying it in a kind of defensive reflex. Let's go back to basics for a minute.

For the public in general, it is only human to be more deeply attuned to bad news. After all, in this century there has been more and more of it. It's untrue that good news is no news--it's just less urgent news. It doesn't threaten or horrify us, and it usually lacks the fascination factor which bad news often contains. Up front and right away, consumers of news simply aren't going to react as viscerally to good news as to bad. Publishers and editors and network news managers know that; their reporters know it, too.

But responsible news organizations run reasonably steady ships. They depict the world as it is, good and bad. True, the prominence given to bad or unfavorable news can be heavily overdone. So can the media's more than occasional weakness for the sensational or superficial. But a news organization that tried to downplay or stifle bad news (or what to you is bad news) wouldn't be a news organization; it would be a fairy tale factory with few customers.

> "...That's been true since Thomas Paine wrote his initial letters. It's a very delicate thing and it's partly what this country swings on, Constitutionally. We tend to err on the side of invasion of our privacy a little bit in the interest of making public the news and the data everybody believes they need."

Even if it were desirable, nothing will ever change this situation very much. The wise federal executive will find a way to manage negative news situations, as discussed further on.

Stay abreast of what's in the press--and what's likely to be.

A senior federal office-holder who doesn't know what the press is saying is asking for trouble. Ignorance in this regard is definitely not bliss. While your agency's press and information operation is a helpful resource, don't depend exclusively on it, or on your colleagues elsewhere in government or your friends to keep you informed. Read the press and keep an eye on what's happening in television and radio--and not just for subjects in your area. If the department publishes a daily or weekly news summary, or distributes one from another agency, read it regularly. When you are too busy to keep up with the news, assign the job to an assistant whose judgment you trust. Ask to be briefed on everything of conceivable concern to your operation.

Some news stories can be unpleasant surprises. If you can't always avoid the unpleasantness, you can often avoid the surprise. Media curiosity can be piqued for any number of reasons, not just the ones you're prepared for. Reporters hear not only about announced activities but often about those--meetings, decisions, travel--that are not made public. Glance periodically at your upcoming personal schedule and the near-term agendas of the programs you're responsible for. Look for items of possible interest to the press and decide what you might do, if they became press stories, to handle them to your advantage or minimize the damage. Maybe there's nothing you can do. Even so, and whether a story is good or bad, you're always ahead if you know approximately what's coming.

Along with knowing the nature of what you're dealing with and how it works, there are a few prescriptions and methods to learn in handling the press:

Get a firm grasp on the different ground rules for talking with the press and the sometimes exotic distinctions between them.

"Well, don't quote me on this, but..." How many times have you heard that familiar request? As a government executive speaking to reporters, you have to pay strict attention to what such warnings actually mean. Do you know the difference between speaking on the record, off the record --and the several shadings in between? You need to.

> "I had an experience when I was at Justice. I was working on an obscure packers and stockyards bill that Congress had...A reporter called. I was trying to distinguish [for him] our position on it, which was an anti-trust position as opposed to the interests of the stockyards. The next day the Attorney General called me in personally. The story was in the [press] clips, headlined 'Inexperienced Attorney Advises President on Veto.' [The reporter] was a Pulitzer Prize-winning guy, and we had sort of said this was for background and not for attribution. Well, I was quoted in the whole thing. That was a lesson."

When talking with a reporter, don't "sort of" mumble about the ground rules. Always specify clearly the basis of your conversation. Make certain that the reporter understands and agrees to it.

The first of these formulas is known universally as "on the record." Whatever you say on this basis can and will be directly quoted and attributed to you by name and position. Reporters favor this framework because it lends authenticity and identified sourcing to their work. News conferences and public speeches are good examples of on-the-record usage. Speakers often use those occasions to make an official point or state an official position.

Next comes "background", in which what is said can be used in direct quotes but cannot be sourced by name and position. The attribution-- "informed sources," or something similar--is anonymous. Background allows the speaker to provide more information than would be possible on the record, and to provide it without being officially accountable. There is a wide acceptance of the authenticity of information, including quotes, reported on background. That makes it a handy device indeed-- for elaborating or defending policy, sending a particular message, express- ing displeasure, even criticizing another government, among other uses. The press dislikes background but accepts its inevitability. And it's often better than no information at all.

If you employ "*deep* background," reporters can include what you say in their stories but must state it on their own--without direct quotes, or any attribution whatever. Select deep background with caution, and only in sensitive situations where it is nonetheless helpful to be able to convey something.

Finally, when you are "off the record," nothing you say can be used at all, in any form. Again, this is a mechanism to be used sparingly and almost always in response to a question. Its chief use is private and confidential--to steer a reporter away from incorrect assumptions and speculation that may lead to inaccurate and damaging stories.

Some old government hands recommend a simple standard for everything said to the press. It is to judge everything you might want to say in terms of seeing it in the newspaper with your name attached; if it wouldn't fly under those circumstances, don't say it. Taken literally, of course, this guideline eliminates any basis for communicating with journalists except on the record. But it does serve as a useful argument for restraint in what you do tell the press, on whatever basis. Using back- ground, for example, may indeed keep your identity out of a story, but what you say could be damaging anyway. And even off-the-record comments have a way of surfacing; a reporter can take what you say off the record and, with skillful questioning, get some other source to say it on a basis which allows it to be used.

The fact is, there are almost no situations in contact with the press-- from talking to a reporter in the office to sleeping with one--where senior government executives can totally let down their hair. It's not that most reporters are malicious, remorseless machines lying tirelessly in wait for an ambush. It's the competitive nature of their jobs, particularly in matters of state; the principles in which many of them believe; and the pressures that drive them.

Most journalists understand the rules of the game and the problems they can incur from abusing them. Government people who know and use the rules fairly can generally expect the same in return.

Handle interview requests judiciously.

> "I would not talk to anybody over the phone for the first time in an interview. You're going to find out how important you are to the story if you insist on meeting."

There are of course many reasons governing your choices of interviews to grant. In deciding, don't neglect the journalists you think have the potential of being useful in advancing your projects or department, or in maintaining good relationships with news organizations you value. Don't, however, play favorites.

If many interview requests come in, get your staff or department public affairs director to screen them for you and--with your approval--make arrangements for those you wish to do.

Don't go into an interview cold.

> "...Be prepared to say something. Don't just go in there with a catcher's mitt, be a pitcher at the same time."

Or, put another way:

> "You should answer the question you wish you'd been asked, not the one you were asked. You have an objective...You shouldn't just go into an interview and respond."

In sum, know what you want to achieve in a press conference or interview. But, however confident you may feel, get help from the career experts in your agency. They have been through it before, and know where to find many of the answers you'll need. If you think you need it, ask for a list of likely questions and suggested answers. If it helps, do a little rehearsing to have some of your own language ready for the main points you want to make.

Tell the truth.

"Stick to one of the following: 'I know the answer
and here it is;' 'I don't know the answer but I'll
find out;' or 'I know the answer but I'm not going
to tell you and here's why.'"

Again, that doesn't quite handle all the possible situations when you're
talking on the record to a reporter, but it's not a bad rule of thumb.
Remember that you control what you want to say, and how much. It's
not necessary to tell all you know about something in order to avoid lying.
But be sure that what you do say is the truth.

Especially on sensitive or troublesome stories, deliberate lying is a
quick ticket to oblivion. Reporters soon find it out, or hear about it from
colleagues, destroying your credibility, your value as a news source, and
your media usefulness to your department. If you can't say anything, or
go further than you already have, there are some safe and neutral ways to
state or convey that fact without any shadings of meaning that you don't
intend. But if you simply don't know the answer or are not informed
about something, play it straight. Say so, and promise to get back later if
possible with the information. Keep in mind that clever deceptions or
evasions are not a cover and aren't appreciated.

Cut your losses.

"If there's a bad story and it's true, step forward
and take control of the situation and explain what
happened...And that's the end of it--it's a one-day
story. But if you let it simmer it will be in the news
day after day."

In other words, the worst way to handle bad news once it is out is to
try to ignore, squelch or deny it. First, analyze the stories and broadcasts
and sort out fact from fiction. Then figure out what you want to say
about it. Next, decide whether to say it without waiting to be asked, or by
responding only if and when the questions come. Either way, explain the
facts forthrightly to whatever degree seems appropriate. Point out any
relevant information that tends to balance the picture in your favor.

As for false and inaccurate stories, don't let them go unanswered.
Only rarely, with stories on subjects like intelligence information or
military operations, will you be unable or unwise to respond. In all other
cases, state publicly and at once that the story is untrue or inaccurate. Be
prepared to show why, if necessary on a background or more private

basis. You can put out a statement, post a notice, talk to the individual editor or reporter, or write a letter to the editor for publication. However you handle it, stay cool.

> "...I have never gotten on the phone and yelled at a reporter--you're not going to undo [the original] story, anyway. But you'll find that, if you do it without raising a big fuss, they will be more careful next time."

> "There's a dignity issue here that's very important...You have to be careful because you'll say things you'll regret. If it's an emotional issue where you can't be objective--if they call your wife dowdy or your husband a drunk--then you should turn it over to your press person..."

Whether bad stories are true or false, don't crawl into a hole and slam the door behind you.

> "These guys are doing their job, and you're not always going to like what you read. But that doesn't mean you shut them off."

Understand how leaks work--and avoid them when possible.

Broadly speaking, a leak is an anonymous disclosure of information with the intention of exerting a specific effect. Usually, it is information that would not otherwise be disclosed in the normal give-and-take between reporter and source; as such, it is important not to confuse it with the use of the background rule. Leaks can be deliberate or unintentional, authorized or unauthorized.

A deliberate authorized leak published in the press, for example, might represent a government effort to sound out the reaction to a policy move that is being considered but hasn't yet been decided on. A deliberate unauthorized leak might be an attempt to discredit a policy or an individual, or simply someone bidding for attention. An unintentional unauthorized leak could be merely a slip of the lip or the irresponsibility of an habitual blabbermouth.

Leaks are yet another fact of life in the media arena. While they can occasionally do more good than harm, things usually turn out the other way around. Leaks regularly produce anxiety or plain outrage in one quarter or another. Just as regularly, administrations vow to do the impossible--stamp them out. It is even more impossible when, as has been true of more than one administration in the past, some of the deliberate leaking comes from the top of the government.

The more successful you are in avoiding the role of a leaker in any form, the better. If you or your actions are the target of a leak, however, don't panic. Decide whether there is a need to respond to it for policy or program reasons; stay away from replying for personal reasons, which can have the effect of confirming whatever the leak alleged about you. Don't respond to a leak with a leak. If you must respond, some of the common sense and advice quoted in this chapter will help.

VIII

ETHICS

Chapter Summary

Be aware that standards exist governing your conduct.

Learn the rules and follow them.

No precaution is too small or too troublesome.

Perception is reality.

If it's in a gray area, don't do it.

One of the first replies given by the President-elect in early January 1989, when the press asked what his initial instructions to his new Cabinet would be, was this one:

> "I'm going to tell them to...adhere to the highest ethical standards."

Less than a week after becoming President, he announced formation of a bipartisan commission to report in six weeks' time its recommendations for new legislation on ethical standards in government. Two days later, meeting for the first time with 3,500 members of the Senior Executive Service, he spoke again about ethical behavior:

> "The guiding principle will be simply to know right from wrong; to act in accordance with what is right, and to avoid even the appearance of what is wrong."

Whatever results from these initiatives and utterances, it isn't surprising that they were prominent in the new President's first words and deeds. In the past generation, episodes of ethical misbehavior have plagued every administration on a generally rising curve, and public concern has kept pace.

On this subject, Watergate and Iran-contra of course leap to mind. But those episodes were extraordinary examples of a different brand of wrongdoing: acts carried out at the highest levels and with a heavily political flavor.

Of equal concern today is the more garden-variety kind of misdeed--a steady succession of violations of conflict of interest and other ethical rules, intentional or otherwise, by a succession of people at various levels of government. Usually, they have sought little more than their own financial or material gain. Some of them didn't even know what the rules were. But their behavior was no less hurtful to themselves and the administrations concerned than the bigger transgressions that capture the headlines.

The cumulative impact of this sad record, plus the lessons of Watergate and Iran-contra, have made the proper conduct of public servants a growing sore point with the press and the citizenry. It's a ticking bomb that no political leader can ignore. Ethics, as George Bush recognized, has become a front-line issue of governance in the United States.

For senior political appointees in government, the most elementary warning in the area of ethics may seem ridiculously obvious. But an old Navy saying insists that "there are always ten percent who don't get the word." For that minority, therefore--and everyone else--let's state the obvious:

Be aware that standards exist governing your conduct.

> "A lot of people just sit in government and never
> know that there are rules, never think about it."

With so much to do, focusing your attention on the ethical quality of how you do it may be difficult. Yet nothing is more important. Nor can anything you do be more fatal than crossing the line of acceptable behavior. And in government as elsewhere, ignorance of the rules is not much of an excuse.

> "I can't believe there is really that much venality
> around--that people would ruin their lives. I really
> believe that they just didn't know what they were
> doing...I would counsel someone coming in to...find
> out from the ethics officer in their agency what the
> rules are."

It will probably be the other way around--the ethics person will come to you before or as you take over your job. Offically called the Designated Agency Ethics Officer (DAEO), this individual is probably a member of your agency's legal staff and will almost certainly see that you are orally briefed on the rules, or receive written material, or both. The DAEO works in close touch with the White House's Office of Government Ethics (OGE), which among other things handles the review of the financial disclosure report that will be required of you before you're nominated, and each year of your federal service. All DAEOs and the OGE operate under the office of the Counsel to the President. Together they enforce the conflict of interest rules throughout the executive branch.

Learn the rules and follow them.

At a minimum, read everything your agency and your DAEO hands you on the subject. Read what the president has said. Beyond those, the National Academy of Public Administration's *Presidential Appointee's Handbook* is particularly informative and readable on conflict of interest and ethical conduct questions.

If you have any doubt about the meaning of a rule or whether something you're thinking of doing may violate it, don't remain ignorant. Again, remember that plenty of expert advice is handy. If necessary, go to the top professional.

> "Every agency has a general counsel, and all you have to do is ask the question."

No precaution is too small or too troublesome.

This applies especially to everyday items--drivers, travel, routine expenses, and the like.

> "Every administration has had problems with this...people who have gotten in trouble for violating some simple rule... For God's sake don't lie to people, don't let somebody pay for a $300 hotel room, don't accept gifts, don't let people buy you lunches..."

Perception is reality.

Avoid the appearance as well as the fact of impropriety. Bend over backward to honor the letter as well as the spirit of the rules, no matter how idiotic it may seem.

> "There were times when I thought it was ludicrous. When I visited ---- Bank, they would offer me a ride to the airport. I would say no--or yes, but I'm going to pay you the equivalent in taxi fare...The question could never be asked whether I rode from Manhattan to JFK in some bank's limousine."

In ethics, once again, the rules may be very different from those you operated with in private life.

> "Anybody who comes from a corporate background...accumulates a certain understanding that you get any number of perks because the corpora-

> tion and the stockholders benefit from the added
> comfort... Anybody who comes from that back-
> ground has to be told that none of that applies."

Still, your mind may be on higher matters, traveling the fast lane of policy and action. Rules about who pays for what in the course of a 19-hour day may not seem like anything to get excited about. The dividing line may look pretty thin--and it's all in the day's work anyway, right? When you think about it at all, your reasoning may seem quite logical and fair.

> "You may be making much less than your counter-
> parts in the private sector and think you want or
> deserve some perks..."

Even if now and then someone else pays for something bigger than just a meal or a phone call or an airplane ticket, so what?

> "That stuff is really the seed of destruction for
> people who have great policy ideas, are wonderful
> managers, but do really stupid things. Maybe it's
> partly the compensation problem, but people have
> got to understand that they have to get their
> personal financial affairs in order, and they have to
> figure out how they're going to afford what they're
> going to do. And then they have to forget about it,
> because it's going to hurt. You've just got to be
> squeaky clean."

A tough problem in this respect--one that has received considerable attention in recent months--confronts the prospective government executive with significant holdings of stock and other kinds of investments. These present obvious potential conflicts of interest that have drawn increasing public concern. Over the years, as a result, stricter rules have evolved for individuals with personal investment portfolios who accept appointment to the federal government.

If you are in that category, consultations with the ethics offices mentioned earlier will in due course determine what is necessary to bring your personal financial situation into line with the rules. Several forms of compliance are available in which you may be faced with some painful choices. It may turn out, however, that you get a waiver: your holdings are judged not large enough to cause conflict; you can keep them and stay within the law. Or you can retain your investments with satisfactory promises to withdraw--recuse yourself--from any matters while in office that might put the public interest in conflict with your own.

The waiver and recusal solutions, while entirely legitimate, should nonetheless cause you to think carefully about appearances. Public perceptions of your position aren't likely to be affected by the fact that you are complying with the rules. You may want to go beyond mere compliance to make clear your belief in the principles the rules embody.

In the last analysis, before you take the job, consider whether you can in fact tolerate the adjustments in financial status which the conflict of interest requirements may call for.

If it's in a gray area, don't do it.

The pressures are always there. The committee chair calls, wanting something done. Or maybe it's the White House.

> "You're pressured to do things--give grants, make statements, give favors--that maybe are on the fringe, not illegal, maybe not even unethical, but certainly unwise."

The answer, of course, is to stop and consider.

> "Visualize the right-hand column of the front page of the *New York Times*. If it wouldn't look right there, don't do it."

> "Looking back on it, I was lucky I took the time to really think about these things. You are paid to say no to people you really want to say yes to. People that you know well, political colleagues. Even the President."

There are also other ways to handle pressure that seems irresistible, particularly if the facts are on your side.

> "I remember one time when ------ was the minority leader and he wanted me to give a grant to a [clergyman] who was running a program...Well, I knew the [clergyman] was probably taking it on the side and it was a lousy program. I refused to fund it, but [the minority leader] kept saying that I really had to do it. So I asked him if I could come up and see him. I went up there, had a private talk with him and explained the whole thing--that he was being taken in and I wasn't going to do this. In the end, he thanked me, because he didn't know

what I knew. He said he appreciated it because
funding the program not only would have gotten
me in trouble, but probably him as well."

In the end, avoiding real or potential trouble in the area of ethical
behavior is a relatively simple matter of constantly examining your own
actions and knowing the rules. In its *Handbook*, the National Academy
of Public Administration sums it up this way:

"The best insurance for presidential appointees
anxious to avoid conflict-of-interest controversies
is to be aware that the appearance of conflict of
interest is as important as the reality, to take the
time to become familiar with the relevant regulations, to complete the financial disclosure forms
carefully and comprehensively, and to consult
whenever in doubt with appropriate government
ethics officials."

IX

LAST WORDS

Enjoy your service in government.

You may have the impression that finding genuine pleasure in an executive job in government is unlikely or impossible. Is it, after all, worth it?

In the experience of most of your predecessors, the answer is a strong yes.

Despite the exasperations large and small, the long working days, the hundred and one burdens to shoulder, and the intense amount of energy and intellectual stamina that these jobs demand, few people regret taking them on. Most of those who have done it express feelings of satisfaction that go well beyond the material gains such jobs may eventually bring-- beyond even the fact of service to the country.

They have found in government, for instance, a chance to expand their knowledge, not merely about their particular areas of specialty and skill, but about the nation and the world. They understand better the problems and promise of government from having witnessed them at close hand. They leave Washington with a better perspective on the country and their own lives in short, with horizons that have been considerably widened.

Getting such true satisfaction from your work is fundamental to any job, private or public. It is crucially important to the quality of the performance you turn in now and later.

Remember that you share the public trust.

Take it seriously. When the country elects a president, it entrusts the nation's business, for better or for worse, to that individual's judgment, skill, honesty, and good faith. When the president staffs the senior jobs in the administration, that trust extends to those selected to fill them.

Each such person must prove that this confidence is well-placed. In its most basic sense, trust is the expectation that you will give the job your best shot, in complete faith with the Constitution you swore an oath to support, and in the directions and according to the policies laid out by the president. That you will do it with the national interest first. And that you will do it with complete integrity.

Those are the true mandates that you've been handed. The details are for you to fill in.